ROAD to
Utopia

Overcoming Life's Challenges

Peter Junker

Road to Utopia: Overcoming Life's Challenges
Peter Junker
© Peter Junker 2024

All rights reserved. No part of this publication may be reproduced, distributed, or transmitted in any form or by any means, including photocopying, recording, or other electronic or mechanical methods, without the prior written permission of the publisher, except as permitted by U.S. copyright law.

Identifiers:
Paperback—9798218470586
Ebook—9798218470593

Library of Congress Number: 2024917201

*To my parents, who instilled in me my faith in God;
To my children, Melissa and Jessica,
who provided joy and happiness in my life; and
To my wife, Monica, a loving partner on our road to utopia.*

CONTENTS

Introduction vii
Chapter One: Polio 1
Chapter Two: Boredom 5
Chapter Three: Priesthood 13
Chapter Four: Shyness...20
Chapter Five: Culture Shock 29
Chapter Six: Life or Death 38
Chapter Seven: New York City Marathon 46
Chapter Eight: French Connection 52
Chapter Nine: Creative Outlets 63
Chapter Ten: Frostbitten 78
Chapter Eleven: Changing Directions 83
Chapter Twelve: Delayering...94
Chapter Thirteen: Love, at Last 105
Chapter Fourteen: Wedding and Honeymoon.............115
Chapter Fifteen: Family Ties..135
Chapter Sixteen: Retirement 141
Chapter Seventeen: Utopia..149
Acknowledgments 159
About The Author...163

INTRODUCTION

THIS BOOK IS ABOUT MY PERSONAL JOURNEY IN SEARCH OF utopia while dealing with and overcoming the challenges that life has thrown at me. Each time I conquered a challenge, it put me further down the road to utopia and made me realize the blessings and miracles that God had and has for me.

Ever since Adam and Eve, life has been filled with pain, suffering and disappointment for everyone. We can either meet our challenges head on or withdraw and be filled with bitterness. My hope is that you will be inspired by my experiences and be able to deal with and overcome challenges as I have.

I wish you blessings on your road to utopia.
Peter

CHAPTER ONE
POLIO

The first challenge I had to overcome in life was the polio disease. I vaguely remember contracting it and gratefully don't remember much of the experience. I was only four years old. My mom and dad told me that my entire right side was paralyzed. The Red Cross picked me up every morning for therapy. I worked with a team of medical professionals and did different exercises to regain the use of the right side of my body. Nurses instructed me to do one exercise after another and keep repeating the pattern until my body hurt. And then do one more. My whole little life was about overcoming this one challenge. It even seeped into how I communicated. I slurred my words and needed to see a speech therapist as the disease gave me a "lazy speech" pattern.

I don't know how long it took to recover, but, miraculously, I regained the full use of my body within a year or two.

Polio was my first encounter with obstacles. And, I didn't realize it at the time, but it was my first glimpse at the love and power of God.

I grew up in a religious household and I'm sure my family prayed for healing over me every day. They shared over the years how scared they were for me. As a little boy, I didn't know I was healed by the grace of God.

Polio wasn't the only obstacle I experienced in life where God played a role in my healing. I nearly died a few times in life, lost a lot of jobs unexpectedly, heartache, and found myself crossing several bridges while running a marathon in New York as a man with gephyrophobia (fear of bridges).

Throughout my life, whenever I was faced with a challenge, I thought back to polio. I was a little boy struggling with a very serious disease and I beat it. It still amazes me that, even if I was only partially paralyzed that I could be cured simply by doing exercises.

Reflecting back on my polio experience, I'd think to myself, with God's help, I can do anything.

As time went on, I also embraced the "power of positive thinking" and "mind over matter." I was able to move my brain, body and spirit in harmony and eventually, intuitively I was in concert with myself.

MY FINAL THOUGHTS

In 1952, there were almost 58,000 cases of polio in the United States that resulted in over 3,100 deaths. By 1954 when I turned four, those numbers had decreased to 38,000 cases that resulted in over 1,300. It was still prevalent in America, and I was lucky to survive it.

I don't know why God heals some people and not others but, in my life, I keep sensing and experiencing that He has a plan for me. I may not know exactly what the plan is but every time I overcome one of life's obstacles, I can feel His presence. I've also learned that miracles can still happen.

NOW YOUR TURN

Can you think of a time in your life when God's grace healed you from a physical impairment?

_____

_____

What is the first memory you have from your life when you overcame a health challenge?

_____

_____

Are you currently facing health challenges in life?

_____

_____

What is your mindset in dealing with it?

_____

_____

Have you prayed for God's healing upon you?

_____

_____

Write a prayer to God below.

_____

_____

CHAPTER TWO
BOREDOM

After Polio, the next major challenge in my life was boredom. I'd bet most young boys experience boredom at some point throughout childhood.

When I was around five years old, I loved to watch the Davy Crockett show on television. Imagine my delight when my parents bought me a complete outfit of his including a replica coonskin hat. It even had plastic fringe on the sleeves and pants. However, one day I was so bored that I ripped all the fringe off it. I still regret doing that to this day.

Even though attention-deficit/hyperactivity disorder (ADHD) hadn't been discovered yet as a disorder, I seemed to have all the symptoms of it. I don't know if this condition contributed to my state of boredom but I'm guessing it didn't help.

When I was in grade school, I would take daily doses of phenobarbital because I was a "nervous" child. Side effects of phenobarbital were severe. Not surprisingly, throughout grade school I suffered from seizures and convulsions.

On my 10th birthday, I had an episode. I was swinging on my swingset in my backyard and I had a convulsion fit. I was really excited to be celebrating my birthday by playing baseball with my friends. However, after I recovered from the convulsion, my mother suggested that I shouldn't play and, instead, be the umpire of the game. I was so disappointed as I had to look on as my friends played without me.

Grade school was a defining time in my life. I had to create challenges for myself to keep myself entertained and occupied. I attended a Catholic school in Pennsylvania and always found myself in trouble. I couldn't get away with anything but I always tried. It seemed like I was caught a lot because I remember numerous after-school sessions where my punishment was writing spelling words on the blackboard over and over again.

Because I was a Baby Boomer, the classroom sizes during grade school were rather large, usually around 60. I liked it when I would sit in the back corner near the wall. I would create a baseball game where I threw a wad of paper against the wall and, if I caught it, it would be an out. If I missed, it would be a hit. I also played football on my desk. I would place bits of an eraser on my desk and roll down a piece of lead from a lead pencil. If the lead reached the bottom in four tries or less, it was a touchdown. If not, it would be the other team's turn.

My best friend was also in my class. We would design baseball stadiums or play games where we would try to remember all the players from a certain team or whose last name started with a particular letter in the alphabet. One day we were doing the latter one when Mother Superior of my 2,500 student Catholic school walked up behind me. She told me to see my nun after class.

My nun told me to take the paper home and show my parents what I did in class all day and have my dad sign it. My parents were very strict, and I was afraid to show them, so I signed my dad's name. That worked until my parents went to parent-teacher night. The next morning my dad woke me up and told me I could go to jail for signing his name.

I loved the cornfield behind our house. In March, the ground was flat. It was a perfect spot to run around and fly a kite over acres of land. I'd race home from school on good kite-flying days, attach a cloth with the perfect weight as its tail and then, go outside and run around for a little while until the kite was afloat.

I would stand there and watch it for a few minutes and then think, *So, now what?*

Of course, I needed to create an exciting challenge so I would let the stick drop with the string around it. I would run alongside it as the wind started to take it away and dive for the stick just as it was being taken into the air. Ninety percent of the time I would catch it. If I missed, I would get a dime and buy another kite.

The farmer whose cornfield was behind our house eventually sold it to a company that was going to build a 50-lane bowling alley. Huge mounds of dirt was brought in and covered a lot of the field. During the Winter, it made for a perfect snow sledding site that was right behind our house! In the Spring, my friends and I designed a baseball playing field. We would play every night after school. It was my favorite pastime and greatly helped me deal with my boredom.

One day, I was supposed to stay after school, but I didn't want to miss playing baseball, so I decided to try and sneak out. There were three lines to leave school: car, bus and walkers. For those like me in the walkers' line, nuns would walk alongside us until we reached a traffic light to cross the street. On this day, my nun was walking alongside the boy who was next to me.

7

We will call him Joey. I couldn't believe it. How was I going to get home without her noticing me? I tried to make myself as invisible as possible and kept looking in the other direction. My mom had aptly nicknamed me "Sneaky Pete" and it worked on this day!

I was so excited until I got home.

My mom was waiting for me at the front door and as soon as I entered, she said, "Weren't you supposed to stay after school today?"

"Yes," I said.

"March right back to school and see your nun at the convent," she said.

My heart sank.

I trudged back to school and found my nun.

"How did you leave school?"

"I was in the walker's line," I said.

"I walked alongside the walkers and didn't see you."

"I was next to Joey," I said.

"I was next to Joey and I didn't see you."

I repeated the conversation she had with him. She still didn't believe me so all I could do at that point was cry, which I did.

After a little while I was able to go home. For the fourth time that day, I walked the mile to and from school. The baseball game was over by the time I got home.

Prior to seventh grade, we moved from a town of around 100,000 to a small town of 2,000 people. Downtown was only three blocks long. It was so boring. There was hardly anything to do. So, as usual, I'd have to entertain myself. I'd make up games with my brother.

I had one brother and four sisters growing up. My brother was a little over six years younger than me. We shared a room and a bed while living here. Of course, we always had trouble falling asleep so we would invent games to play. One game was called "Spy." To get to the bathroom, we had to walk past our parents' bedroom. The floor squeaked in spots and my mom was a light sleeper and we didn't want to wake her up. The idea was to get to the bathroom and back with as few squeaks as possible. The winner would be the person with the lowest number. Occasionally, my mom would wake up. If it was me walking, it would have been no problem because I was a lot older than my brother. However, if it was my brother, he would get in trouble for not being asleep yet so either he would try to imitate my voice, or I would throw my voice out there and shout, *It's Peter.* Either way, I believe it worked every time.

Another game we would play was Radio. I would be a human radio and my nose would be the channel turner. I would provide news, weather, sports results, commercials and even music, depending on which channel he chose. If he didn't like one, he would twist my nose and another one would come up. Little did I know that, years later, I would work as a DJ at the campus station in my first two years of college.

During the day, to entertain myself, I'd create challenges. Mostly in the form of stealing.

At first, it was just cherries off a neighbor's tree. Then I would swipe produce that a local grocery store would put out on the sidewalk.

Once stealing fruit became easy, I challenged myself again. A friend of mine told me about a tavern that had paper tattoos wrapped around a piece of gum. One day I walked right into the tavern and past the barkeeper to the end of the bar where I saw the box with the gum and tattoos. Without a word to anyone, I put my hand in the box, grabbed a tattoo and walked right out of the place.

It was 1962 and life operated differently. I only went there a few times but it was memorable. I quickly graduated to the candy store. Candy became my favorite thing to steal.

It was paradise for children and candy lovers alike! When I walked in the store, there was a middle row with candy on both sides. There were also rows of products along both walls heading to the back of the store. At the very back was another row perpendicular to the other three and that's where the cashier stood. I preferred to steal from the middle row.

One day, I took some candy and, when I went outside, had it in my right hand wrapped around my bike handle. When the owner came out, she asked me if she could help me with anything. I told her I was fine and was just looking. My heart jumped in my chest as she took my left hand off the bike handle!

I tried to look as innocent as possible but was certain she would take the right hand next, and I would go to jail. But she didn't. Instead, she said that the next time I come in I better buy something or don't bother coming in the store. She walked away and I rode off, very relieved.

To this day, I don't know if I got lucky or if she knew I had it in my right hand and was just trying to scare me into not stealing. Either way, I never stole anything from anywhere again. I was cured of the habit.

MY FINAL THOUGHTS

While I hated staying after school and writing spelling words on the board, I later became very adept at spelling and won numerous spelling bees. I even came in third place in the state of Michigan in my Senior year of high school.

My boredom is still with me today. For example, as much as I enjoy watching football on television, it is difficult for me to sit still for long periods of time. My preference is to tape games so that I can fast forward through commercials and any periods of inactivity.

I think boredom is a condition similar to depression. It's not something that you can cure with drugs or alcohol. The way to homeopathically treat it is to find enjoyable activities and/or to create challenges. I love being challenged and having the opportunity to conquer challenges. When I play a game, I prefer losing a close match than winning in a dominant manner. My goal is always to challenge myself to do the best I can and keep getting better at a particular activity or skill.

NOW YOUR TURN

Do you find yourself bored in life and looking for ways to feel something different?
_____
_____

Are you challenging yourself in healthy manners?
_____
_____

What do you do when you find yourself bored in life?
_____
_____

Would you rather win a game by a large amount or lose a close one?
_____
_____

Are you able to sit still for long periods of time?
_____
_____

What are some ways that you entertain yourself when you're bored?
_____
_____

CHAPTER THREE
PRIESTHOOD

My parents wanted me to become a priest from the day I was born, October 4th. My birthday happened to be a feast day in the Catholic Church for St. Francis of Assisi. Therefore, my middle name is Francis in his honor. My first name is Peter, and my Confirmation name is Joseph. Talk about pressure. Try living up to Saint Peter, Saint Francis, and Saint Joseph as you go through life.

There is nothing wrong with being a priest, however, it was hard to know if that was my calling when I was seven or eight years old. I didn't know what I wanted to be when I grew up. I loved playing baseball and hanging out with my friends. But, I considered priesthood. I showed a little interest in understanding the saints and that's when my parents encouraged me to be an altar boy. I was in second grade at the time.

I felt special. It was like being in a play. I put on a special garment, had special duties with water and handing the priest wine. I felt important. I was the second hand to the main guy in charge on Sundays. At least at our church. And, since Mass was in Latin, I had to learn a foreign language that I would only speak once a week. Latin came easily to me. But, occasionally, I forgot a line and the priest would lean over and whisper what I was supposed to say.

I felt the blood rush to my cheeks when I'd make a mistake. I felt guilty for making mistakes but when the priest bent down to correct me, I had to stifle a laugh.

Some masses required the burning of incense. I didn't mind the smell of incense. All Catholic Churches use them. It was my job to place the incense in a thurible, a metal container with a lid that had holes throughout and hung from a long chain.

Once I got the incense lit, I blew on it to get it really smoky and then handed it off to the priest and he blessed the altar and congregation with it. I loved it. And, considering I had a little obsession with lighting things on fire at the time, I really looked forward to serving during those masses.

There was one occasion where I was serving at a very special Mass that included the Archbishop of Philadelphia. I'll never forget when we were in the back getting ready and he told me to watch what he does when the priest is not around. He proceeded to take the incense burner and swung it around like a lasso! I was stunned and knew that it would be forever etched in my mind.

When I was in eighth grade, an opportunity to get out of class came up. I could volunteer to serve at funeral Masses which were usually on Fridays. Since school was boring, I jumped at the chance to do something different, not knowing if I'd enjoy or even feel comfortable serving at a Funeral Mass.

It was a big mistake. It was so hard seeing and listening to people cry over their loved ones every week. I soon regretted my decision and asked my nun if I could withdraw from

Funeral Masses and come back to class. Gratefully, she let me. I didn't volunteer for anything else after that.

At the end of eighth grade, an award was given to the top two girls and boys with the best grade point average for the first eight years of school.

To my surprise, I received an award for having the second-highest grades for boys. My parents were so happy. They always pushed me to do better in school, especially my dad. If I came home with a 95 percent on a test, he asked why I didn't get a perfect score.

"Did anyone get a perfect score," he'd ask.

"One boy," I'd say.

"Well, if someone got a perfect score, then you should have been able to get one too."

I was thrilled to receive an award for two reasons. The first was that my nun was unsuccessful in her attempt to give awards to only girls. She hated boys and always put us down. If it were up to her, boys would never be awarded. Gratefully, that didn't happen.

The second reason I was so happy was because my grades were high enough for my parents to send me to a highly rated high school called Devon Prep. It was an all-boys school, and my parents thought if I wasn't surrounded by girls, I wouldn't be interested in them and might fulfill their dream of me becoming a priest.

I was accepted at the school, but never attended. Before high school started, our lives went down another path. My father's company decided to merge some divisions and his division was eliminated and he lost his job. So, my dad went back to his first love, which was teaching, and landed a position as a Professor at Ferris State College in Big Rapids, Michigan. At the time, Big Rapids was a town of about 8,000 people, an hour North of Grand Rapids.

Alas, for my parents' sake, the only high school in town was co-ed so I was surrounded by girls. It didn't take long for me to realize that I had a different calling than the one my parents wanted me to have.

By the time I got to high school, the Mass was spoken in English and the priest and altar boys faced the congregation. Even though Latin was no longer used, my parents still insisted that I take two years of Latin in high school. I guess this was in case the Church decided to go back to Latin later when I was a priest. Other than learning a few catch phrases like, *Veni, Vidi, Vinci* (I came, I saw, I conquered), *Amor Vincit Omnia* (Love Conquers All) and *In Vino Veritas* (In Wine, There's Truth), the only good it did me was when I worked on crossword puzzles. I wish that I would have taken a language like French, especially since I later visited France a couple of times.

When college came, I went to Ferris State College for my Freshman and Sophomore years. My father was a professor there and tuition was inexpensive.

I lived at home and could walk to campus as it was just down the street. I joined groups on campus and got involved to experience as much of college as I could. I realized I needed social education as much as I needed academic education. I needed to grow.

I became a member of the Newman Club. This was a club for Catholic students. I became President in my second year. The "Folk Mass" movement was happening in the late 1960s and we embraced it. Music at Mass was usually of the Folk variety and played on guitars instead of an organ. I, along with two others, played at these services. One day, the other two people were sick, so I had to perform solo. You won't ever see or hear me on "The Voice" as I'm not a good singer. I'll never forget on this one particular Sunday that I started playing and singing faster and faster on "They Will Know We Are Christians By Our Love", or maybe by how fast I played.

After transferring to another college in New York City for my Junior year, I was on my own for my first time in life. Life was different. I grocery shopped for myself, could sleep in if I wanted to, stay up as late as I wanted to, go out whenever I wanted to. It was total freedom. I didn't have anyone looking over my shoulder.

And the more I leaned into my new freedom, the less interested I became in doing anything I felt obligated to. And attending church was one of those things. As a result, I lost interest in the Catholic faith.

It took another 35 years before I decided to accept Christ and became a Christian. Once I did, I decided to use my creative talent to write a sermon. My Church agreed to allow me to present it one Sunday. I thought my mom would be excited that I would be preaching, even if it wasn't as a priest. She asked me what I would be wearing. Since I lived in Hawaii at the time, I said an aloha shirt with dress slacks. I guess she was still hanging on to her dream of me being a priest because she asked if I would be wearing a white collar.

While I never did become a priest, I'm glad that I was able to minister to her later in life. I would call her every weekend to chat.

One afternoon, she told me she didn't know where she was going when she left the earth. I was able to share with her how God sent His Son Jesus to die for our sins so that we would all go to Heaven when we died. She recited the Sinners' Prayer with me and accepted Christ. I now look forward to joining her in Heaven one day.

With my sisters' help, I was able to video chat my mom during the last week of her life. At the beginning of the week, I told my mom, "I just want you to know that I love you, Mom." Her final words to me were, "So, what, you didn't love me before?" She had a sense of humor til the very end. At the end of the week, she couldn't speak but could hear. I called her one more time and told her I wanted to sing a song to her. I pulled it up on my phone and started singing, "I'll Fly Away." She immediately started singing along with me as best as she could. I struggled singing it while crying simultaneously.

MY FINAL THOUGHTS

I think if God had wanted me to become a priest, my dad never would have lost his job and then have us move to Big Rapids, Michigan where I attended a co-ed high school.

I liked the challenge of learning Latin in second grade and later in high school. I wish it could have been more useful in my life. I believe my role as an altar boy provided me with acting/stage experience which would come in handy later in my life. My experience with the archbishop taught me that life is too short to take seriously all the time.

When I became a Christian, I learned that the difference between it and Catholicism is that Catholicism is about what you must do to be saved, whereas Christianity is about what Jesus did to save us. Although I'm no longer practicing the Catholic religion, I'm glad for its spiritual concepts of a Christian nature that were instilled in me.

NOW YOUR TURN

Do you know what your calling in life is?
_____
_____

Is it something that you feel inside you or something that others have told you?
_____
_____

What do you believe your purpose in life is?
_____
_____

In what areas do you want to focus your attention?
_____
_____

Do you have a faith you're practicing? And, what is your next step to furthering your faith?
_____
_____

CHAPTER FOUR
SHYNESS

I REMEMBER AT THE AGE OF FIVE BEING EMBARRASSED TO GO outside to get milk when I was in my underwear. The girl next door, also around my age, just happened to come outside at the same time. This would not be the last time I would be shy around a girl.

My shyness lasted all the way through high school and my freshman year of college. When I was growing up, I was hypersensitive, and this led to my condition. I believe I was this way due to living in an overly disciplinarian environment. It was not uncommon for me to go to school after being yelled at by my parents at the breakfast table. It was a terribly depressing way to start the day.

I was also teased and bullied quite often by other children. They made fun of my last name even though it was pronounced *Yunker*.

There was a TV commercial at the time for a candy bar called Chunky. Their tag line was, *Open wide for Chunky!*

Of course, classmates changed the line to, *Open wide for Junky*! I was also known as *Junk* and other variations.

When I was still in grade school, I decided that I would change my last name when I got older. However, for some reason, I decided to look it up in the dictionary.

Junker with a small "j" was defined as: *An old car in poor condition.*

To my amazement, it was also shown with a capital "J" and was defined as a: *Young, German nobleman*, and *as a member of a class of aristocratic landholders.*

I later discovered that airplanes were also named after that family. These were the Junker 87 and Junker 88 (JU 87 and JU 88). Since I realized that I had nobility in my blood, I scrapped my plans to change my name later in life!

When I was in eighth grade, some boys in my class thought it was cool to walk up behind me, reach down between my legs and squeeze my testicles. I didn't think it was very funny. Once, when a boy did this to me, I turned around, got him in a headlock and started racing towards the school wall.

Fortunately, I let go about three feet before getting there but his momentum carried him into it, and he hit his head. The damage was a lot less than it could have been. Even though I was responding to what happened to me, I was the one in trouble with everyone.

Now, other classmates wanted to beat me up after school for causing harm to that boy. As soon as the school day was over, I got out of there and ran. I hid behind some trees until I saw my classmates pass by. They were out looking for me but didn't see me that day. Just another day in the life of an eighth grader.

Another time during recess, someone tapped me on the shoulder from behind. I turned around with the intent of hitting whoever it was. However, it was my mom who was helping out at school that day and I nearly belted her! Yes, paranoia ran deep for me during those years.

By the time I entered high school, I was at my fourth school in nine years. It made it harder to make friends, especially, because of my fragile emotional state. So, except for a few bright moments, I generally hated high school.

I counted down the days until graduation! When I look back at photos taken at my graduation party that my parents threw, I have a sad, expressionless look on my face. You would think that I would have been delighted that it was finally over. I think my look captured the four years of Hell that I internally endured.

It had worn me down so much that I couldn't smile, even knowing that I was now starting anew with fresh opportunities to finally enjoy life.

Music helped me get through high school. I loved listening to it, and it was exploding in unprecedented creativity in so many ways. It also captured my feelings with songs like, "*I Am a Rock*," by Simon & Garfunkel which described living inside the walls you have built around yourself to keep out pain.

When I wasn't in class, I would sit on a bench in the hallway and watch the other students go by. I would imagine what it would be like to be friends with them. I was basically living inside myself.

One day, when I was walking to class, a girl came alongside me and grabbed my arm like we were walking together. Everyone laughed! I wanted to become invisible and disappear. I wanted to be like Alice in Wonderland and crawl down a hole but there was none. So, I just went to class and sulked.

I was attracted to many girls in my grade as well as some in other grades. The problem was that I was too shy to get to know them and give them a chance to know me. I'll never forget my Dad telling me when I went to a school dance to make sure to dance with the ugly girls because they like to dance too. Little did he know that I was too shy to ask any girl to dance, regardless of what she looked like.

In my freshman year, there was a girl I liked but, of course, she had no way of knowing it because I never said anything to her.

One day she came into one of my classes with a note from the principal for our teacher. I was sitting in the front row and immediately blushed and dropped a pencil on the floor. I proceeded to stay under my desk until she left. How embarrassing!

In my junior year, there was a girl I liked who struggled in Math. That was my best subject, so I brilliantly offered to help her. We met after school in the library where I tutored her. It was the most exciting part of my day! It was the closest I came to going out on a date with someone until Senior year. I don't know if I was able to help her all that much, but these were some of the happiest moments of my high school years.

In my Senior year, I finally got up the nerve to ask out our foreign exchange student from Denmark. She was cute and very sweet. I still don't know what gave me the courage to even talk to her. Maybe I was tired of sitting on the sidelines. I'll never forget our first date. We went to see "Guess Who's Coming To Dinner," a movie with Sidney Poitier in it about a white girl bringing home her black fiancée for the first time. The movie came out in 1967 so it was quite radical at the time. Since it was my first date ever, I was very nervous and for conversation said, "I would still go out with you, even if you were black." To make matters worse, when I walked her to the door, I asked her if I could kiss her good night and she said, "No."

Overall, I enjoyed my first dating experience with her, but I don't think she did. In my yearbook she wrote: "Since you forced me to write, I will. Good luck with yourself, your friends and your parents. You need it. Do not always be good, that is no fun. But you will probably never realize it." Oh, well.

After basically living in a cave during my four years of high school, I finally emerged and welcomed a whole new world when I started college at Ferris State. I was now one of 8,000 students and found it a lot easier to be myself. I was free to come and go as I pleased, take whatever classes I wanted to and dress however I liked. Since I had my own car, it gave me an even greater sense of freedom.

One of the appealing things about attending Ferris was that they had a campus radio station, WFRS. When I was in high school, I would daydream about being a DJ at the station since I loved music so much. I even decided that my on-air personality would be "PJ the DJ." They didn't take just anybody, and I had to apprentice before hopefully getting voted in. Fortunately, I made it and was thrilled to have the opportunity to spin records. We played records from a "Top 40" music list but, during Finals week, we could sign up for blocks of time and play whatever we wanted.

Sometimes, I would play all "British Invasion" groups like the Rolling Stones, Dave Clark Five, Animals, Kinks and, of course, the Beatles. Other times, I would play all R&B, especially Motown and then American groups like the Beach Boys, Mamas and Papas and Simon and Garfunkel.

Working at the station was also the first step in overcoming my shyness. I told myself that there was no such thing as a "shy DJ" and realized that no one could see me so I could just be myself when I was on the air. It also helped that sometimes women would call me and tell me that I had a sexy voice.

I applied for a job with the Michigan Department of Transportation after my freshman year in college. The job required traveling around the state during the Summer and stopping motorists to take traffic surveys. My interview was in Midland. I was a little concerned because my uncle had lived there once and was caught embezzling money from a car dealership. The interview seemed to go well until the very end when the interviewer said, "I just have one more question. Are you any relation to... (I held my breath) ...the Junker 87's and 88's (JU-87 and JU-88, German war planes). I breathed a sigh of relief and said, "Not that I'm aware of but I have heard about them."

Whew!

Ferris State ended their Spring session two weeks later than most colleges so when I arrived, there was already a camaraderie among the other guys. I wanted to fit in so when they acted all macho and talked glowingly about how girls were attracted to them, I did the same thing. Little did they know that I was the exact opposite as I only had three dates my freshman year and two of them were blind dates. The facade worked until one day...four of us decided on our day off on July 4th to go to the sand dunes to meet girls.

I was terrified as I sat in the back seat on the way trying to figure out how to keep my cover from being blown. I decided the best thing to do was to keep pretending I was somebody else.

I also prayed that there wouldn't be any girls around. Alas, when we came over a hill, there were two girls sitting on a blanket. The four of us had split up so there was one for each of us to talk to.

I wracked my brain and the most brilliant thing I could think of to say was, "Hi, my name is Peter."

She smiled at me and said, "Hi, my name is Nancy."

At that moment, all the tension and nervousness just melted away and from some unknown source I was able to speak coherently in an articulate manner.

Words just flowed from my mouth and with each one I could tell Nancy was more interested in me. This was my social epiphany! It was like a superpower had been unleashed in me! It definitely was the next step, and certainly the biggest step, in my social development. I call it my Summer of Awareness. The rest of the Summer shone brightly as a great weight had been lifted and I was no longer socially insecure.

Later that summer, four of us were walking down a street when a carful of girls in a convertible started yelling and honking at us in a favorable way. Since we were all young boys, you would think that each one said that the girls were yelling at them. Surprisingly, when we got back to the hotel with the other guys, they all said that the girls were yelling at me! This positive reinforcement further added to my personality development in overcoming shyness.

After my Summer of Awareness, my sophomore year in college was socially hyperactive. Every weekend was filled with dates, parties, sports events and other activities. I felt like a superhero who had just realized a secret power. I was finally getting the social education I needed to go along with my academic education. I'll never forget how, after a few months of this whirlwind activity, my mom asked me, "Peter, you used to stay home every Friday and Saturday night and watch TV with dad and me, but now we never see you. Why not?" I sheepishly replied that I was spending them with my friends and offered no other information. In retrospect, they probably knew exactly what was happening with me.

MY FINAL THOUGHTS

We form our identities based on both positive and negative experiences. Early in my life, they were negative and contributed to a low self-image. As I grew older, the positive experience helped me improve my self-confidence. Eventually, I cared less about what others thought about me and focused on who I wanted to be and the life I wanted to have.

High school would have been a lot more fun if I had the courage to be myself and let others get to know me, especially the girls. I would have had a social life and grown up sooner and not have been such a "late bloomer." I also learned that my sense of humor was a great mask to wear when I was nervous on a date. It calmed me down and made me at least appear to be somewhat normal. The irony is that years later through attending class reunions, communicating on Facebook and playing Words with Friends with some of my female classmates, I've built great friendships with many of them. Learning this lesson the hard way is one of the biggest regrets in my life. Finally, I did learn what it took to have fun.

NOW YOUR TURN

Did you have to overcome shyness in your life?

If so, how were you able to do it?

If not, what can you do to overcome it?

Do you realize that being shy is a reflection on how you feel about yourself?

Name one person you would love to have a conversation with and what's holding you back from not communicating with them yet?

What's the worst that could happen if he/she doesn't want to engage with you?

CHAPTER FIVE
CULTURE SHOCK

When I was a Senior in high school, the Guidance Counselor asked me what career I had in mind. The idea of being a priest crossed my mind when I was younger but once I grew out of that, I never questioned what I'd be as an adult.

I told her that I wanted to be a baseball player. I loved baseball. I played on a team every summer and looked forward to it. My Guidance Counselor asked me if I was good at baseball. I wasn't a good hitter. I was a good fielder. But, I told her no to be on the safe side. She then suggested I consider a different career, something I enjoyed and something I was also good at.

I let that sink in and every once in a while I'd wonder about it.

I liked Math and did very well in it. My parents were aware of my grades and pushed me to do better. My dad traveled for his job a lot and if there was some math-related gadget at a conference, he brought me home one. I remember sitting down at the kitchen table and learning how to use the slide-rule.

One day, my dad brought home brochures of different math-oriented careers and encouraged me to read through them. I had a few choices: Become a teacher, a mathematician or an actuary. I decided on becoming an actuary because it was interesting, challenging and rewarding. My next thought was, *wait, that means I have to work in insurance! How boring!*

My Dad convinced me that since the first two years of college basically included General Education courses, I might as well go to Ferris State College (now University) which was three blocks away. I could learn about different interests and explore other fields. Plus, my dad also taught there, and it was relatively inexpensive.

Then, after two years, I could transfer to a school with a good Actuarial program. That was the plan and I proceeded to fill up my schedule with only Math and Business courses during my first two years. I didn't think an Actuary needed to know Science or a Foreign Language.

My hope was to transfer to the University of Michigan which had an excellent Actuarial program. The school was willing to give me a grant, scholarship or whatever financial aid I needed since my grades were excellent. However, the Admissions Department would not accept me because I hadn't taken language and science courses.

My next attempt to transfer there was to apply to the School of Business within the University of Michigan, but they wouldn't give me credit for the Business courses I had taken so I didn't have enough credits to transfer. I thought most colleges would be like this, so I decided my best option was The College of Insurance in New York City. I didn't think they would care if I had taken language and science courses, and I was right.

The College of Insurance (TCI) was a work-study school. This meant that I would alternate between attending school for four months with working for my sponsor for four months. The college was founded by major insurance companies in the 60s due to a lack of college graduates looking to work for insurance companies or even having any training in the subject of insurance. Each of us had to apply for and have an insurance company sponsor us.

Crum & Forster agreed to sponsor me, and I worked in their Actuarial department. They paid for two-thirds of my tuition and books. If I continued working for them for at least two years after I graduated (which I did), they would reimburse me for the other one-third of my college costs.

This turned out to be a major turning point in my life.

Not only was I about to leave a town of 8 thousand people and move to a city of 8 million, I was doing it alone. My parents were happy I was accepted to a University and had a great career path and I was ready for a new adventure and a chance to spread my wings. It certainly was an adventure getting to New York as it included a 24-hour train ride from Kalamazoo, MI to Croton-on-the-Hudson, NY. The trip was interrupted twice. Once, we had to stop near Detroit as someone put a shopping cart full of bricks on the track. Then, we stopped again somewhere in Canada when a passenger didn't have a ticket or enough money to buy one.

Since my dad was a college professor, he was friends with other professors. A colleague of his had a daughter, son-in-law and grandkids who lived in upstate New York. So, it was arranged that I would stay with that family and ride the train and subway down to school. I was grateful and felt blessed that I was staying with people who knew the area.

However, not only was I now in a different geographic location but the cultural environment was different. The town of Pleasantville where I was staying and the family I was staying with were upper class whereas my family and the town of Big Rapids where I came from were middle/lower class. There was a certain air about everyone and everything that made me feel like I was in a movie, sort of like The Stepford Wives. It didn't seem real.

The family had certain routines that they followed. The husband would have a vodka tonic each night when he came home from work. Sunday nights were always game nights as we played charades and we ate toast with cheese slices on top. It was cut into thirds. I only had classes on Monday through Wednesday so I had a four-day weekend every weekend. However, the wife made me get up at 7:00 a.m. each Thursday and handed me a list of chores to do that day. I didn't mind doing chores for the pleasure of staying there but I didn't understand why I had to get up so early.

My first impression of New York City (the City) was on the train ride from Pleasantville. It went through Harlem, where I saw people with a depressed look on their faces just staring out their windows. I felt so sad for them. It was the exact opposite of the bucolic setting of the Rockefeller Estate that I would pass on my way to the train station in Pleasantville.

After departing the train in Grand Central Station, I came across a scene that looked like a horde of cockroaches all scattering about when the light was turned on! Then I had to squeeze onto a subway train and forget about being nice and letting others go in front of me.

The subways were noisy, smelly and had a dangerous air about them. Big Rapids did not prepare me for this! Once I reached my subway stop, I exited and was engulfed in the largest mass of people I ever had encountered. To make it less daunting, I pretended to be a running back and would look for holes to dart through while walking to school.

When I arrived at TCI on my first day, I felt totally lost and I was a little overwhelmed as I was in a foreign environment and wondered what was in store for my future. Little did I know the transformation that awaited me.

I chose to attend TCI with hopes of earning a Bachelor's of Science degree in Actuarial Science. Therefore, most courses I took included either insurance, math or business. Some of the insurance courses I took were Risk & Insurance, Property & Liability and Principles of Ratemaking. Math courses included Statistics, Calculus and Differential Equations, the hardest math class I have ever taken. Finally, business courses included Business Law, Government & Business and Principles of Finance.

Fortunately, I was able to take a couple of elective courses that had nothing to do with any of the above. One was "Contemporary Theatre." Every week, we would attend a different performance either on Broadway, off Broadway or Shakespeare in the Park. Our homework assignment was to write a review of each one.

I love the arts and enjoy writing, so I was able to get an "A" for this class. It was also enjoyable to see all the different kinds of productions in various venues. I particularly enjoyed Shakespeare in the Park because of its setting and, of course, the guy wrote some good plays. Having taken this class opened the door for an opportunity later in life after I graduated.

Another elective course I took was Pioneers of Modern Painting. We studied all the Impressionist artists. These included Monet, Renoir, and Cezanne, just to name a few. We also studied Van Gogh who is considered a post-Impressionist artist. In addition to being a break from insurance and math classes, I took the class for two reasons. I thought it would be an easy "A" and the teacher was pretty, sexy and only a few years older than me.

I didn't realize that I would fall in love with these artists, particularly Monet. I think I was also distracted by the teacher because I was only able to get a "B." Still, it was one of the most interesting classes I have ever taken! Whenever I travel, I always visit museums, when possible, and see the original works of art up close. More about them later.

Since my sponsor, Crum & Forster, was located in northern New Jersey, it would have been a terrible commute to get there from upstate New York where I first stayed on my arrival. I decided it would be wise to find an apartment that was also located in northern New Jersey. It would have been extremely difficult to go through the City each time I went apartment hunting so I decided to live with another family that we knew back in Levittown, PA, the town where I grew up.

The family owned a sporting goods store and I helped out there in return for room and board. It was actually enjoyable as I love most sports and it was great to be surrounded by sports equipment and help sell it to customers on behalf of my hosts.

Levittown was northeast of Philadelphia and required a two-hour commute to school. This included driving to Princeton Junction to catch a train to Newark, NJ and then a subway into the City. This experience taught me that I could do almost anything if I knew it was only temporary. Fortunately, it didn't take very long to find an apartment in Parsippany, NJ which was only a ten-minute drive to where I would be working.

There were only a handful of women attending TCI when I was there. None of them held my interest. It was difficult meeting women while going to school because I spent most of my free time commuting. I was usually unshaven to a degree and wore a t-shirt and either jeans or shorts, depending on the time of year.

Part of my journey included riding the subway which didn't seem very safe, so I didn't mind looking like the poor college student, which I was. One day, I was riding the subway to school and there was a very pretty lady standing next to me. She was well dressed and wore nicely scented perfume.

My brain kept saying, *no way could she be interested in me, especially with how I looked.* However, my instinct kept getting signals that told me otherwise. I told myself to wait and see if she talks to me. If she did, then I would know she was interested. Finally, she asked me if I had the time. That's all I needed. From then on, the conversation flowed freely.

She told me her name and gave me her number before we departed. At the time, I lived in Northern New Jersey, and she lived out on Long Island, but I happily made the drive to spend time with her one Sunday afternoon. Everything felt right about our time together, walking and talking, riding bikes and sharing laughs.

I was in my early 20s at the time and the thought of getting married one day was the farthest thing from my mind. But, after our time together, I started to think that it might be a possibility someday. However, when I called her the next night to set up another date, she told me that she decided to go back with her boyfriend. I was crushed but the time spent with her made for a memorable moment in time.

I experienced some of the coldest and rudest behavior in my life in New York. I'm not saying everyone there is like this but there definitely was a much greater negative aura there than anywhere else I have lived or traveled to. People were constantly pushing and shoving to get on to subway trains.

When I asked for change at a newspaper stand since I needed exact change to get on the subway late at night, I was told, "What do I look like, a bank?!"

When I politely asked for a little mustard from a hot dog stand to put on my hot pretzel (Philadelphia custom not followed in New York), the response was an emphatic "No!"

I was also constantly in fear walking around the City, especially at night. I realized that I needed to learn some street smarts quickly to survive the jungle. I constantly checked when crossing alleys and I was always looking over my shoulder.

MY FINAL THOUGHTS

My experiences in New York City were not all negative. I loved Central Park, a giant oasis of grass, trees, and streams in the middle of a concrete world. Since I had developed an appreciation for art, I enjoyed going to museums like the Metropolitan Museum of Art, the Modern Museum of Art and the Guggenheim, a museum where you start at the top and walk down a spiral pathway to the bottom. There were many others as well. Of course, concerts, plays and musicals also fueled my creative interests.

I believe that the City was where I first nurtured my love of food and became a foodie. My first experience with interesting and delicious Greek food was in The Village section of the City. The feta cheese, kalamata olives and spanakopita were all delicious!

There were plenty of Italian restaurants to choose from and eating at them felt like I was in Italy. One such place had a bocce ball court along tables in one room where you could play while waiting for your food. La Fondue restaurant was a treat as you could have cheese, steak or mouth-watering chocolate fondue!

NOW YOUR TURN

Have you ever been to New York City?
_____
_____

If so, what are your positive and negative feelings about it?
_____
_____

Have you ever traveled to a large city/metropolitan area after growing up exclusively in a rural area?
_____
_____

If so, what was that experience like?
_____
_____

Do you have a preference for living in either a rural or urban area? If so, why?
_____
_____

CHAPTER SIX
LIFE OR DEATH

THE TOUGHEST AND MOST IMPORTANT CHALLENGE IN LIFE is staying alive. Aside from medical setbacks, there are circumstances sometimes beyond our control that could end our lives abruptly. I experienced numerous situations like this.

Living in the Midwest, I was familiar with wild weather.

In April of 1967, I was a Junior in high school in Michigan. One day, I was sitting in my Algebra II class when I noticed outside the class window that wind was kicking up dirt from the nearby practice football field. Other classmates also noticed, and the teacher became upset with us and told us to pay attention. A few minutes later, the tops of the trees were bending over and touching the ground.

At that point, the teacher told us to all get under our desks. Michigan averages 15 tornadoes a year and we usually get tornado warnings or tornado watches. This time, there was neither. We could hear the loud destruction as the tornado tore the roof off the school. Fortunately, no one died or was seriously injured but the whole scenario was extremely alarming. Afterwards, there was the calm after the storm as it was extremely peaceful walking home from school.

A few years after that, I found myself diving into a ditch to avoid death.

I worked for the State of Michigan Highway Department during the Summer after my Freshman year in college. We would travel around the state and stop motorists taking traffic surveys. One day, we were on a freeway that had a 70mph speed limit. We were all wearing bright orange vests and hard hats. We took turns standing in the fast lane with a bright orange sign that read *SLOW* and pointed the drivers to the lane to be surveyed.

I was not too excited about being in this position and my fears were soon realized. A vehicle was approaching me as I pointed them to go into the next lane. As they kept getting closer without changing lanes, my brain wondered if they would run me over just to avoid stopping. The answer was "Yes!" and I barely had time to jump into the ditch before my life ended!

And then years later, also on the highway, I found myself in another life or death situation.

I would drive back home to Michigan from New Jersey during college term breaks and usually take 13 hours to travel the 800 miles. I graduated from TCI in December and was looking forward to going home and sharing presents and the Christmas spirit with my family. However, the trip at this time of year presented a few obstacles.

For starters, I threw a graduation party for myself the night before I was supposed to leave. Of course, my excitement trumped my self-control and I overindulged. When I woke up the next day, I was greeted with blizzard conditions. This meant driving at 25 mph instead of 60 or higher. To make matters worse, my heater didn't work.

A sensible person would have just gotten it fixed and then made the trip. However, in being overconfident in my resourcefulness, I decided that I could make the journey by drinking coffee to keep my body warm and smoking cigarettes to keep the car warm. I would exit the freeway when the cold became too overwhelming.

I was able to maintain control this way for about 100 miles. It was miserable and uncomfortable. When I realized my body was shivering and it seemed like it was weakening, I knew I had to get off the highway and find a way to warm up. Through the blizzard, I could see the next exit ahead was only ¼ mile. I could feel my body shutting down more and more each moment. It was vital I get out of the cold so I sped up and went as fast as I could. I immediately lost control of the car and started heading for the ditch. I stopped the car before it reached the ditch and got out of my car and tried getting someone to stop.

I could feel my body rapidly deteriorating and kept saying to myself, *why doesn't anybody stop? Can't they see I'm dying?!*

Finally, a car did stop, and the family inside let me sit in the back seat for a while until I was comfortably warm. I was so grateful. I sat there for twenty minutes and jumped out and kept on driving.

I immediately drove to the nearest hotel and checked into a room. I took a hot shower and laid under as many blankets as possible, but I kept shaking. Eventually, I warmed up and fell asleep. When I awoke, I found a mechanic to fix my heater and then proceeded on my journey home. When I finally arrived home, my family was sitting around the dinner table. Such a welcome sight!

However, no sooner did I start to eat than my dad told me that "Your mother says that if you don't agree to get a haircut while you're here, you can just turn around and go back."

Really?! Are you kidding me?!
I was stunned and simply ate my meal in silence.

Later, while I sat in my old room contemplating my choices, my dad came in and asked if I had decided yet. Because of my desire to enjoy the Christmas holidays with my family and give them the presents that I so thoughtfully purchased, I agreed to get a haircut but promised myself that this was the last time I would give in to them.

After college I spent a little more time in New York but eventually moved out to Southern California.

On April 29, 1992, I was working in downtown Los Angeles on Wilshire Boulevard. At 3:15 PM that day, the Rodney King verdicts were announced that acquitted all four Caucasian officers of Assault and three of them with Excessive Force for the severe beating of King after a high-speed chase ended. Almost immediately, the city erupted with riots breaking out everywhere. More than 60 people died and over 2,300 were injured. When the verdict was announced, my supervisor told all of us to leave at once.

I couldn't believe my eyes when I pulled out of the parking lot. It looked like a war zone, and I had to maneuver through an obstacle course to get home. There was gunfire and people being pulled from their cars. I was petrified and didn't know if I would make it home safely. When I finally got home, I packed up the family and we headed West for an hour to Ventura to stay there until things calmed down. We didn't come back for six days.

Southern California had wild weather just like Michigain but instead of tornadoes, we had earthquakes and there were no warnings.

I was living in Culver City, CA, a suburb of Los Angeles on January 17, 1994, when I was abruptly awoken at around 4:30

AM due to an earthquake lasting around 20 seconds. The epicenter was 60 miles away in Northridge, CA but it felt so strong that it seemed like the epicenter was next door. The original magnitude was 6.7 and two aftershocks followed at magnitudes of 6.0. Nearly 60 people died and more than 9,000 were injured.

I experienced numerous earthquakes during my 25 years in Southern California, but this one was unlike any other. For one thing, after most earthquakes, things would normalize within a few hours except for some occasional aftershocks. I was expecting to go to work later in the morning until I noticed on the news that the 10 Freeway, a major thoroughfare, had collapsed.

When earthquakes occur, my first thought was that I hope the building doesn't collapse. My fight-flight-freeze response kicked into high gear immediately. I never wanted to look outside the window out of fear of what I'd see and what damage I'd be looking at. It seemed like they would most often occur early in the morning, usually when I was sleeping. This made it difficult to maintain your equilibrium and one time I fainted due to this.

Sometimes incidents that threatened my safety ended up being comical in the end.

One day, I was taking my wife to her doctor's appointment for issues with her knees. She was standing by the car while I was bringing her wheelchair from the house. We were running late so I was in a hurry and pushed the wheelchair quickly. It hit a bump in the sidewalk which caused me to fly in the air and do a somersault.

Fortunately, I landed on my feet, but my momentum was bringing me forward and I was afraid that I would fall on my face. I tried to run as fast as possible to keep that from happening but, eventually, I fell. I was able to land on my right side and only bruised my shoulder and rear end.

I looked up at my wife's face and she was stunned. I was in pain and grateful it wasn't worse.

Another time, I was horseback riding along the beach in Georgia. We had to go through a forest to get there. My horse kept giving me problems with obeying my commands. On the way back, she was headed towards a hole which I thought would cause her to fall. I tried to steer her to the right, but she kept going left. Suddenly, my saddle started shifting to the right and I could feel myself falling. My fear was that she would then stomp all over me so as soon as I hit the ground, I rolled rapidly to the right. Fortunately, she missed and, again, I bruised my shoulder and rear end. Thank goodness they are both a little meaty. Ironically, when I was little my parents never let me ride horses out of fear that I'd have a convulsion on one and fall.

I've experienced my share of life-threatening occurrences and illnesses. Beating polio as a young child was a miracle and God's grace. And years later, when I tested positive for COVID in May of 2022, I prayed for the same grace.

Older people with comorbidities were more susceptible to experiencing the worst side effects of the disease, including death. I was extremely concerned as I was 71 and suffered from hypertension and diabetes. Fortunately, because of my situation, I was able to be admitted to a hospital the next day and receive a monoclonal antibody intravenous treatment. I was able to leave at the end of the day and proceeded to work from home for a week. My symptoms included congestion and overall fatigue, but they lessened each day. Finally, I recovered and tested negative and was able to return to work.

MY FINAL THOUGHTS

Life is extremely fragile and can be taken from us in a matter of seconds. When we are young, we tend to think that we are immortal and act in foolish ways sometimes. Hopefully, we live through our poor choices and learn from our near-death experiences.

When natural disasters occur, we hope that we are not in the wrong place at the wrong time. When I walked the streets of New York City, I was always very mindful of my surroundings and quite often looked over my shoulder. I apply the "street sense" I learned there whenever I find myself in large crowds where one can be most vulnerable.

Resourcefulness and survival skills are also necessary tools to acquire. Finally, I believe strongly in God's plan for each of us and I think He will take you when He believes your time has come. Because of everything I have survived, I think He still has plans for me here on Earth.

NOW YOUR TURN

Have you ever had a near death experience?
_____
_____
_____
_____

If so, how were you able to survive it?
_____
_____
_____
_____

Do you believe that God has a plan for each of us?
_____
_____
_____
_____

Do you live each day like it could be your last?
_____
_____
_____
_____

CHAPTER SEVEN
NEW YORK CITY MARATHON

One October Sunday, I happened to watch the New York City Marathon on TV and decided that would be my next challenge.

I never ran track in high school but won some races as a freshman in my college Physical Education class. I composed a training schedule covering the next 12 months leading up to the race. On my first day, I merely ran around the block and nearly died! Gradually, I improved my stamina and distance.

During the Winter, I ran two miles in 20-degree weather with snow on the ground. I was bundled up and used sweat socks for gloves because they breathed better than regular gloves. I learned that running causes your body temperature to rise so it wasn't as bad as I thought it would be.

By April, I was running seven miles around a track in the early morning before work. Birds would be chirping, and I would imagine that they were cheering for me. I initially thought that running that much before work would tire me out, but it had the opposite effect as it got my blood flowing.

Early in the Summer, I increased my running distance to 10 miles. There were a few times that I experienced a runner's high at that distance. Eventually, I increased my distance to 12 miles. I had hoped to run at least half of a marathon, or 13 miles. However, I didn't know at the time that my feet would overpronate when running and I needed orthotics to correct it. I kept getting shin splints and faced a dilemma.

I wanted to increase my distance even further to get as close to 26 miles as possible, but it didn't seem likely. So, I made the decision to run 10 miles or less while training and then just do the best I could on race day. I learned in the past that my determination was strong, and it helped me accomplish a lot of goals that seemed unreachable. Bring on the marathon!

The weather in New York City for running the marathon in late October is usually cool with temperatures in the 60s, which made it ideal for running 26 miles. However, it was 85 degrees and without a cloud in the sky on the day that I ran in it. It was so hot that, in addition to handing out cups of water, helpers also gave us ice cubes. I held them in my hand and sometimes rubbed them on my neck to try and keep my body temperature down. To make matters worse, the race that would go through all five boroughs started on the Verrazano Narrows Bridge that connected Staten Island with Brooklyn. I had a phobia about crossing bridges and there were five of them throughout the race!

Surprisingly, where the race started turned out to be a good thing because the numerous helicopters above us picked up cool air from the water below and made the starting temperature bearable. Once we got into Brooklyn, the weather turned hot again, and it was surprising to see Hasidic Jews standing on the sidewalks wearing their heavy wool garments.

When I was training for the race, I decided to find a pace that I thought I could run all day. It turned out to be a 10-minute-mile pace. If I kept it up for all 26 miles, I would finish the race in about 4 1/2 hours—not bad for the first time running it. Everything was going according to plan as I kept up that pace for the first 13 miles, or half the distance. However, at that point, my knees were killing me from running on cement for over 2 hours, so I stopped to walk.

As soon as I did, my thighs, hamstrings, and calves tightened up. At that point, I decided to continue with a combination of running and walking. I was about ready to quit at the 19-mile mark but since I was just entering the South Bronx and the police escort had passed me by, I realized I wasn't in a safe place to stop. I kept going.

Once I got through the South Bronx, I entered Harlem and I still didn't think it was a good idea to stop there so, again, I kept going. Fear is a powerful motivator. Finally, I made it to the entrance of Central Park with only three miles to go. Once I entered the park, a young black boy riding a bike came alongside me and offered me a beer. I appreciated the offer but declined because I thought it would be better to wait until I finished the race. I also thought it was ironic that I was concerned about running through black neighborhoods because I didn't know how safe it was and here was a black person offering me a drink.

There were one million spectators lined up across the entire route and still quite a few hours after the race started when I entered Central Park. One was a beautiful woman who gave me a great big smile and cheered me on. That also helped motivate me to finish the race. Eventually, I did, and it was the greatest feeling in the world even though my body was wracked with pain. As a four-year-old, my body was partially paralyzed with polio and now, I had just completed a 26-mile race!

MY FINAL THOUGHTS

Take advantage of opportunities to do the things you love. Running is a very uplifting experience. It's not just physical, it's also spiritual as you get to know yourself better and find that you can exceed self-imposed limits on your abilities. Birds are my friends! Exercising before work makes it easier to get through the workday. You can get high naturally. Anticipation is a powerful motivator.

The race served as a lesson about how to achieve my goals. First, ignore how difficult it might be to achieve something and, instead, focus on the goal. If I thought about how hot it was, how many bridges I had to cross, how my body felt when I stopped walking, etc., I never would have finished the race. I just kept focusing on what I wanted to accomplish and did it.

Second, it's important to break down large tasks into smaller ones. When I ran the race, I broke it down into five-mile segments and congratulated myself on reaching each milestone and entering Central Park. If I kept thinking that I had to run 26 miles, it probably would have seemed too daunting of a task.

Finally, I realized that "With God, nothing is impossible," Luke 1:37. Yes, I had polio as a child and there were numerous roadblocks to completing the race, but my faith was strong, and I know that I could not have done it without God's help.

NOW YOUR TURN

Have you ever had to tackle a project that required a "marathon" effort?
_____
_____

If so, were you able to stay focused on the goal and not get sidetracked by how difficult it was?
_____
_____

Were you able to break it down into smaller segments to make it seem less daunting?
_____
_____

Do you believe that anything is possible if you just "put your mind to it?"
_____
_____

Do you believe that all things are possible with God's help? Do you have a huge task at hand that you can ask God to help you with?
_____
_____

CHAPTER EIGHT
FRENCH CONNECTION

My high school friend, Jack, spoke eight languages fluently. He received an offer to teach French sailors on the Riviera how to speak English. He invited me to visit him while he was there.

My challenge was that I knew very little French.

Oui.

Bonjour.

Merci Beaucoup.

And, Voulez-vous Couche Avec Moi, Ce Soir, which meant "Would you like to spend the night with me?"

The opportunity to visit France far outweighed any hesitancy I had plus Jack would be my translator.

Beth, my roommate's fiancée, was in Paris studying her Ph.D in European History. She had an apartment in the heart of the city and she, and my roommate, graciously agreed to let Jack and I stay with her during our one week there.

It was a great deal for both parties. We took her to lunch and dinner and, on alternate nights, she cooked us a gourmet meal with the ingredients we had purchased at the farmer's market. Back then, we could get a 5-course meal including wine for around $20! Europeans ate later than Americans are accustomed to, usually around 8:00 p.m. or later.

Because of our late dinners, we weren't that hungry when we woke up the next day so we would stop at a crepe stand on a nearby corner for a light breakfast consisting of homemade crepes with a choice of a variety of fillings, both sweet and savory.

Another time, we visited Jack's cousin who was around 50. She served us a delicious boeuf bourguignon with Mouton Cadet wine that was so smooth and intoxicating. I had to laugh when I heard Jack's cousin giving him grief because he was speaking French slang. In fact, he was so good with his accent that even the locals thought he was French!

One day, Jack announced that we were going to a movie that night. I was quite surprised that, with all there was to see and do in Paris, we were going to do something that we could easily do back in the States. Then he checked the listing in the newspaper and said we had to get there early to see the commercials. Again, I was surprised because that's one of my least favorite parts of going to the theater.

Of course, he knew what he was talking about because the commercials were European and totally different from anything we see in the U.S. After about 5-10 minutes of showing them, the lights came on and girls with trays of the items that were advertised walked around the theater selling them to the patrons. A treat!

Then we started to watch, "*That's Entertainment!*" I started laughing, almost immediately. When Jack asked what was so funny, I said that "I didn't know Frank Sinatra could speak French."

Since we were in France, the entire movie was dubbed for residents to enjoy and it didn't even cross my mind that people in France would be able to watch movies made in the United States.

Quite often, just the two of us would laugh out loud while witnessing something that only an American would understand and see the humor in it.

The only radio station in France at the time was Radio Monte Carlo. It came on every night at 6:00 and they would play an eclectic mix of songs, everything from opera to country to rock to blues to gospel, etc. I always enjoyed listening to the first song they played every night. It was "*Jessica*," a long instrumental by the Allman Brothers. Years later, I would name my second daughter that name and whenever I heard her name, it would remind me of the wonderful time I had in France.

Like most European cities, looking at the architecture in Paris was an adventure in itself. Beauty surrounded us, everywhere we looked and down every road we walked on. From the doors to the rooftops, I loved looking at the buildings. The beauty of the city forced us to slow down, take our time, and really embrace the art of sightseeing. Everywhere I looked, I saw Roman figures and gold inlays, beauty in simple brickwork, and elaborate designs.

The most iconic structure, of course, is the Eiffel Tower. My first sight of it was on a cruise down the Seine River. However, my line of sight was photo-bombed by the Statue of Liberty! What was that doing there?! Of course, Jack, my translator and tour guide knew exactly the answer.

The original statue was a gift in 1886, from a French sculptor, Frederic Bartholdi to the United States, commemorating the alliance of France and the U.S. during the American Revolution. In return, the American community gave a fourth of the size replica to France in 1889, to commemorate the centennial of the French Revolution and it sits along the Seine.

Back to that other structure, the Eiffel Tower is as breathtaking as it can be and has a very magnetic personality. I couldn't stop looking at it! Elevators took us up to all the levels where I got a panoramic view of the city.

I stepped off the elevator and walked out onto the terrace, wrapped around the top of the Eiffel Tower. The view took my breath away. I paused to soak in the magnificent surroundings. I was staring at a city built thousands of years before and felt grateful for the opportunity.

Since Jack and I were only in Paris for a week, we made sure to visit the big tourist attractions each day. After the Eiffel Tower, we continued on to the one of the most famous cathedrals in the world.

No trip to Paris would be complete without a visit to Notre Dame Cathedral. It sits majestically on the Ile de la Cite on the Seine. It is a mass of architectural fusion with a spire pointing towards Heaven, iconic twin towers, numerous shapes and sizes of windows, including some stained glass, and gargoyles guarding it from high above.

The inside is brilliantly lit and brings its majestic beauty to life. My attention was immediately drawn to the main altar which displays the famous Pieta sculpture by Nicolas Coustou, flanked on both sides by statutes of Louis XIII and Louis XIV. Its multitudes of archways give it a sense of awe-inspiring strength.

Notre Dame overwhelmed me with its artistic beauty. I also felt a strong spiritual connection when I viewed the Pieta, a sculpture of the Mother Mary holding Jesus after His crucifixion. I had seen a photo of it many times while attending Catholic grade school and now I was seeing it in person. I also learned that it was dedicated to the Virgin Mary and that Notre Dame stored a religious artifact of the crown of thorns that had been placed on the head of Jesus during His crucifixion.

Once we got our fill at Notre Dame, we went to the most famous museum in Paris called the Louvre. The entryway features a glass pyramid in front of a centuries-old building with stunning architecture. It's a perfect juxtaposition of architectural styles. I was in awe and in love with everything from the buildings to the art inside. The interior was filled with an array of great art including Coronation of Napoleon, Liberty Leading the People, the Venus de Milo and its most famous work of art, Mona Lisa.

I knew a lot about the painting before we went to the museum. I imagine most people have read or learned about the Mona Lisa. I stood in front of the painting, among hundreds of others, and waited to feel excited. Instead, I felt let down. The hype of her bemused smile didn't live up to reality. The painting measures only 21" x 30" and she is placed behind glass. The glass was placed there in the early 1950s after it was damaged by a visitor who poured acid on it. Since then, there have been several other unsuccessful attempts at vandalizing it.

A few days later, after a lunch that included a lot of wine, Jack and I were walking down a street when we spotted middle-schoolers playing basketball at a playground. As basketball aficionados, we asked if we could join them. They readily agreed and wanted to play a game against us. Thinking it would be as easy as scooping chocolate mousse, we said, "Oui!" What we didn't count on was that there were six of them and only two of us.

Operating under the "We don't need no stinking rules" theory, they jumped on us whenever we had the ball. To make matters worse, they had a "female Jerry West" on their team with deadeye accuracy. We tried to run fast breaks, but in our condition were rather sloppy at it. We played to 21 with one point for each basket. Despite our impaired condition and feeling like Gulliver surrounded by Lilliputians, we somehow won 21-19.

I love Impressionist art and Monet is my favorite artist. I couldn't wait to see his water lily murals at the Musee de l'Orangerie. They were displayed in two rooms, one each on 8 walls. He painted them how they would appear throughout the day from sunrise to sunset.

There were also other paintings by him and his fellow Impressionist artists. We planned on going there on our last day in Paris before heading to the Riviera. Unfortunately, that was on a Tuesday, the only day the museum was closed. C'est la vie! I vowed to return one day just to see Monet's works of art in this museum. It took 42 years, but eventually I did return and found them to be as stunning as I had imagined!

The next day we took a 4-hour train ride to Toulon on the French Riviera. This is where the naval base was where Jack taught sailors how to speak English. It was a fascinating journey as we traveled through beautiful countryside. Occasionally, we would see a small, self-contained village, like you see in the movie, "Beauty and the Beast."

If we had planned it, we would have gotten off the train near them just to absorb their enchantment. Once we arrived, we had lunch at an outdoor cafe. It was so overwhelmingly surreal that I exclaimed, "Here we are, Jack, having lunch at an outdoor cafe on the French Riviera. It doesn't get any better than this!"

The thought occurred to me when I knew I was going to France that maybe I would meet a French woman. I had been smitten with them ever since meeting one in Montreal during Expo '67. When we got to Toulon, there were days when Jack was unable to join me as he had to work. On one of those days, I met Catherine, and my wish came true.

She filled in for Jack as my tour guide and French language instructor. She showed me the sights in the area. We went to the beach and dined at cafes together. It was great conversing with her except when she preferred to speak French and I had no idea what she was saying. I tried to learn but I preferred that she speak English since her English was light years better than my French. Our relationship wasn't any more than this, but I was delighted whenever I was in her company.

As in Paris, whenever Jack and I would dine at an outdoor cafe, it was so surreal that I would again say, "Here we are, Jacques (improper translation) and Pierre, eating at an outdoor cafe on the French Riviera!" We also frequented the cheese shops (fromageries) to discover cheeses that had never graced my palate before. Since there are over 400 different types of cheese in France, we could try a new one every day for a year and still not exhaust the possibilities.

There are eight different types:

- Pressed
- Pressed and Cooked
- Goat
- Blue
- Processed
- Soft with Natural Rind
- Soft with Washed Rind
- Fresh

Additionally, we visited bakeries (boulangeries) and sampled croissants, eclairs, macaroons, crepes and madeleines. It was also on this journey that I discovered a fondness for Beaujolais, a light and fruity red wine. It was also very reasonably priced and, after I returned to the states, was able to buy it for $5 a bottle for many years.

One day, neither Jack nor Catherine were able to join me for lunch. I thought it would be a good test of the French I had learned regarding food items, so I went by myself to a local cafe. After the waiter welcomed me and asked me what I would like, I said, "Bonjour monsieur, jambon et fromage baguette avec beurre." (loosely translated: ham and cheese sandwich on baguette with butter).

The waiter understood everything I said except beurre (butter). I tried saying it about 10 different ways, but he still didn't understand. So, I got up, walked into the kitchen, opened the refrigerator door and pointed to the butter. He said, "Oui, monsieur, you want beurre (with a better French accent than me)". I thought "that's exactly what I said." I went back to the same cafe the next day and when the waiter saw me, he said, "Bonjour monsieur, jambon et fromage baguette avec beurre?" When I said, "No, I think I want something different today," his face just dropped!

I tried ordering a meal in French again and it went about the same as the day before. This time though, I didn't have to walk into the kitchen and point to an ingredient.

One of Jack's friends had a car and offered to drive us along the Riviera on our last weekend there. We gladly accepted! The main road that runs along the Riviera has a mountain on the left as you're traveling East and a cliff on the right. There is not a lot of room for error. You would think that most drivers would drive cautiously given this predicament, but you would be wrong.

It seemed like everyone had a sports car like a Maserati or Lamborghini and drove them as fast and as recklessly as possible! One time a driver decided to pass four cars around a blind curve. If another car had been coming around the turn, we probably all would have been dead. I used to think that New York drivers were the worst but, after this experience, it's definitely the French!

Our first stop was in St. Tropez. We went to the beach, and I spent the whole time looking for Brigitte Bardot. If I were a filmmaker, I would have written a movie called "Looking for Bardot", a la "Waiting for Godot". Alas, she was nowhere to be found. I guess she didn't get the news that I would be there.

We continued our journey through Cannes and then stopped at Nice for the night. Of course, we all couldn't resist saying "Nice was nice" over and over again. We stayed in a hotel three blocks from the beach. It cost each of us $20. I remember saying that "We could stay in a hotel in Cleveland for $20 a night" as we appreciated our good fortune. The next day we drove through Monaco, Monte Carlo and eventually to Menton, on the border between France and Italy.

We ate at an Italian restaurant there. I was amazed that everything was cooked in front of an open hearth with a burning fire. There was no timer or temperature gauge. It didn't matter if it was pizza, pasta or something else. I discovered two unusual pizzas when we were there. One had seafood on it and the other had fried egg on each slice. Now, when I get up and there is leftover pizza, I warm it up and put fried eggs on it.

They had a jukebox and a song I liked was "Long Tall Glasses" by Leo Sayer. It struck me that the title had little or nothing to do with the song and mentioned it to Jack. Of course, he said, "Name one." My mind raced furiously since I was an ex-DJ and didn't want to get embarrassed. I thought of the Beatles songs and songs by The Rolling Stones and other artists. It just wasn't coming to me…until…I said, "A lot of instrumentals are like that". Touche!

MY FINAL THOUGHTS

As I reflect on the three weeks I spent in France, at that time, it was the best vacation I ever had. I learned so much about their art, architecture, food, wine, language and culture. I thought I had become adept at least being able to order in a restaurant but, when I got back to the states the only word I recognized was "avec" which means "with". So, the entrees were always "something with something".

I wish I had studied French in high school instead of Latin. I discovered that the Mona Lisa was small in stature and behind glass. I found out that there was a replica of the Statue of Liberty on the Seine. I saw villages in the country that were many hundreds of years old. I loved their cheese so much that when I returned home, I immediately enrolled in a "Cheese of the Month" club! I'll never forget sitting at an outdoor cafe on the Riviera and taking in the surreal experience. The memory is forever etched in my mind.

NOW YOUR TURN

Have you ever traveled to a foreign country?
_____
_____

Was it difficult to navigate if you didn't speak the language?
_____
_____

Did you make any new friends in the foreign country?
_____
_____

Did you learn about the country's people and their culture?
_____
_____

Will you go back there again?
_____
_____

What did you learn about yourself there?
_____
_____

CHAPTER NINE

CREATIVE OUTLETS

I BELIEVE THAT GOD GIVES EACH OF US TALENT(S). I THINK the way to thank Him is by using the gifts He gave me to the best of my ability. One of my God-given talents is creativity. When I find myself with an opportunity to be creative, I can feel God working through me as it just flows out of me. The challenge for those of us who have this talent is finding outlets to express it. Fortunately, I was able to find many areas of my life where I could apply my talent.

The earliest that I can remember using this talent was when I was in grade school. As I mentioned, I would create games while in class to fight my boredom. This included my version of baseball and football. Also, my friend and I would design baseball stadiums. Later, when I was in eighth grade and my brother was in first grade, we would play games at night when we couldn't sleep like Spy and Radio.

Although I was very quiet and shy in high school, it served as a breeding ground for my creativity. I think being sensitive fueled that ability. I used to read a book of limericks by Ogden Nash. Nash would write things like: "The cow is of bovine ilk; one end is moo, the other, milk." Inspired, I then proceeded to write my own limerick: "Age is as irrelevant as ears on an elephant."

In retrospect, it would have made more sense to substitute "a tail" for "ears." However, what's amazing to me is that I discovered this concept at such a young age, and it is still reflective of how I feel today, considering that my mind thinks I'm 10-20 years younger than I really am.

For years, the Junior Prom was held in the cafeteria. Then, one year, they decided to move it to the gym. I don't know why this bothered me so much since I still wasn't dating and had no plans to attend the event. But it did, so I wrote a satire that our school newspaper published.

I described a couple entering the gym and used a metaphor of them playing one-on-one basketball. I used basketball terms that could also apply to dancing like *guarding her closely, spun around,* and *dragged his pivot foot,* etc. Eventually, the boy stepped on the girl's dress, and they fell to the ground and immediately started wrestling. This time I used wrestling terms that could also apply. The match ended when the boy got a *pin* and fixed the girl's dress.

Considering my shyness, I was amazed that I even tried out for the Senior Play, "The Man Who Came to Dinner." Even more amazing was that I was selected for a role as a doctor. In one of the scenes, I dropped my bag, and everything fell out. I was taken aback when the audience roared with laughter. Of course, the next night, I hammed it up a little and it wasn't as funny.

One night after rehearsal, a friend and I were fooling around with the color lights backstage. I noticed that it created a psychedelic effect. This proved to be useful later. The school held a One-Act Play Festival every year. To be considered, I had to take a speech class. There was no way that would ever happen because I was so shy. If I wasn't in tune with the entertainer within, I didn't like attention. Then, in my Senior year, they waived that requirement, and anyone could enter a play.

Since it was an election year, I decided to write a play about the candidates running for President that year. It was called "A Funny Thing Happened on The Way to The White House." I spent five months writing it and I wrote it in the "Meet the Press" style of candidates being interviewed. It included people like Ronald Reagan and Timothy Leary who I had running on the Let's Stop the Democrats (LSD) ticket.

Little did I know that Leary did run for President in California. I remembered the color lights flashing and did that when Leary came out with "Purple Haze" playing in the background. He was immediately swarmed by hippie flower girls who threw flowers to the audience.

This was also the year that Lyndon Baines Johnson (LBJ) decided not to run for re-election. However, when I wrote the play, it was performed prior to his announcement. My neighbor looked a lot like LBJ, and he agreed to be in my play. He wasn't introduced as a candidate, just as a passerby. He was included in a "Man on The Street" interview in the last scene. A reporter asked him who he would vote for in the upcoming election. His response: "I like Johnson, he's my type of man."

I cast my classmates to play various roles in my play. I asked the class clown to play Ronald Regan. I asked the class fox to play Timothy Leary. He was surrounded by flower girls. I cast the prettiest girls in my grade to play flower girls and the valedictorian to be the reporter.

Three of us produced plays for the festival. My play that I wrote, directed and produced went on second. The audience loved it. They were still in a humorous mood when the next play came on. The play was of a very serious nature but the audience couldn't help laughing at inauspicious places.

After I graduated, a publication called *Spectrum Magazine* was looking for a Theatre Critic. Because I had taken the theater class in college and had experience writing reviews, I was hired for the position. The position didn't pay anything, but it provided an opportunity to obtain writing credit. Since I would be attending dinner theaters, it also included free meals. Ever since I wrote, produced and directed a one-act play in high school, I've always enjoyed going to the theater. It was a great outlet for a creative interest of mine.

The opportunity got even better when the magazine approached me and asked me to be their Sports Editor. That too was a free position but since I was always a big sports fan and, at this time, especially interested in basketball, I accepted immediately! I received a Press Pass and had free admission to New Jersey Nets' games. I also had access to food and beverage that could be consumed before the game, at halftime, and after the game.

The greatest appeal was that I would get to interview some of my favorite players, like Dr. J, and Coach Loughery after the games. I had to remind myself to act like a reporter rather than a starstruck fan. Alas, I never did get the opportunity to meet my favorite player of all time, Pistol Pete Maravich. That would have been special.

Another positive was that I had a phone interview with Arthur Ashe, the tennis great. He told me that there was too much emphasis on children becoming professional athletes and there needed to be more focus on educating them so they could be successful later in life.

After I moved to Los Angeles, creative opportunities abounded. I met a young lady who was a very talented singer. I gave her advice on music choices and basically acted as her manager. I thought she could go far. We dated for a few years and I produced a music video with her in it to promote both her as a singer/performer and myself as a video producer. Each day of the video shoot, I would play "*Flashdance*" by Irene Cara to inspire and motivate myself before going to the location.

Since the video was called Voodoo Doll and had jungle scenes, I wanted to film it in Arcadia, California where Fantasy Island was filmed. However, we would have had to provide evidence of a $1 million liability policy which would have cost a minimum of $1,000 and the budget could not provide that. I met this challenge by finding a nursery in Tarzana, California and we were able to create a jungle setting by filming in front of a hanging vine.

Later, I discovered that the nursery was the former home of Edgar Rice Burroughs who wrote the Tarzan stories, which explains the town's name. Coincidentally, I later directed a video shoot of a charity event in East Los Angeles where Herve Villechaize was the main attraction. He played Tattoo on the Fantasy Island show.

I was a big fan of WKRP in Cincinnati which was filmed near where I lived in North Hollywood. I sent them a script for a show that featured Bailey Quarters as a DJ. Nothing came of it. Then an insurance colleague told me one day that her college roommate was an actress in Los Angeles. My first thought was that there were thousands of actresses in the area. However, then she told me that her friend had a guest role on WKRP, and I should call her up and meet her as she was in the phone book. That got me excited, and I followed through on it. After we met, she arranged for me to attend the show and meet the producers to set up a meeting with them.

When I went backstage, I found myself standing next to Loni Anderson. I was afraid to say something stupid, so I didn't say anything at all. Finally, she turned to me, held out her hand and said, "Hi, I'm Loni Anderson" (as if I didn't know). My brilliant response was, "Hi, I'm Peter Junker". That was the extent of our communication, and I was too shy to ask her out on a date.

When the show was finished, I was introduced to the producers. The conversation went great and it led to a sit-down meeting to discuss ideas in depth later. They really liked one of them for a "John Lennon Tribute Show" but, unfortunately, the show got canceled soon after.

One of my friends during this Hollywood period was a background singer for Bette Midler. Although we dated, I didn't consider us a couple but my friend did. She was good friends with Irene Cara. Irene was filming a movie called City Heat starring Clint Eastwood and Burt Reynolds. My friend was invited by Irene to be on the set on the last day that Irene was shooting a scene. My friend asked me to join her. We initially sat just off the set in a bar area. My friend told me that she had a couple of drinks with Clint Eastwood the night before. When Clint came by our table, my friend introduced us, and I very cleverly told Clint, "You're a tough act to follow."

Later, we sat on the set in the middle of a barroom scene. The actors were over in one corner. When the scene ended, they walked past our table where five of us were sitting. Burt Reynolds came up to me, held out his hand and said, "Hi, I'm Burt Reynolds." My response was, "Hi, I'm Peter Junker."

He had been sick for a while and I asked him how he was doing. He said he was now good, and he learned that being sick is a great way to lose weight. I found it interesting that the only two celebrities who introduced themselves to me were Loni Anderson and Burt Reynolds, who would later marry each other.

Once Irene was finished shooting about ten of us went out to dinner. I sat at one end of the table next to my friend and across from Irene. Irene kept paying me compliments and telling me things like, "You're so cute!" I repaid them and really wanted to ask for her phone number, but since my friend considered us as a couple I was afraid of what might happen if I dared ask Irene out, so I didn't. At least, I did share with Irene how I would play her song each day while shooting a video.

I was a national finalist in a songwriting contest I entered with a song called *"Don't Make Eyes."* The song included the following lyrics:

> You take me out to many fancy places
> But all you do is check out the other girl's faces
> Had I known you were gonna roam
> You could have left me sitting at home
> Because being with you is like being alone
>
> Don't make eyes, do it on your own time
> Why should I suffer on the inside
> Don't make eyes, don't make eyes, don't make eyes

The singer I managed at the time introduced me to a young man who later changed his name to Keb' Mo'. Keb' offered to put music to my lyrics and he helped me record a demo so we could interest other artists to sing it. We became great friends and he went on to stardom as a contemporary blues artist who has won Grammys and numerous other awards.

My biggest excitement was when I worked for a TV show called "Music Video Network" on CBS. I picked the videos to be shown, wrote patter for the hosts that would introduce them and then helped edit the final version. After shooting video all day of the intros, everyone would go home except the Producer and myself.

We then went to the editing studio, but the Producer couldn't pass a bar without stopping. Once we got to the studio, he proceeded to snort lines of coke. He asked me how I would edit every segment and I wound up editing the whole show. I should have gotten Producer credit for the show but, at least, I did receive Writer credit. The show was canceled when it was discovered that non-union help, including me, was hired.

After that show got canceled, I was offered the role as an Executive Producer with a new cable company, Pacific Coast Network, in Burbank. I would have the opportunity to create shows. It would have been a great creative outlet for me, but, unfortunately, one of their investors backed out and it never got off the ground. After three wonderfully exciting years in entertainment, I decided it was time to get a steady income again and go back to insurance.

Before I left California, I worked for a large insurance broker. One of the benefits of working for them was that they had a Toastmasters Club. I knew I needed to improve my public speaking, so I joined. It also provided an outlet for my creativity as I would approach each speech as a mini production. Each of the first ten speeches focused on improving one aspect of speechmaking.

For the speech on utilizing vocal variety, I imitated Julia Child and proceeded to explain how to make goose liver pate. In her high-pitched voice, I started by saying "Today, we are going to make goose liver pate. First, you kill the goose!" I noticed that people were laughing at my jokes during my first three or four speeches. I purposely input as much humor into my next speech and decided that if the audience responded in a laughing manner that I would then hit the stage! They did and I enrolled in a stand-up comedy writing and performing class.

My first performance was at a bar in Huntington Beach, California. My routine made light of shows like: The Bachelor and Joe Millionaire and Wife Swap. Several of my friends and co-workers came to the show. My supervisor even showed up. Much to my surprise, it went well, especially considering that it was my first time. The routine was three minutes long. There was a red light on stage that would blink when one minute was left.

After three minutes, it would blink constantly until you left the stage. When my time was up, I was on a roll and still had more material. There was no way that I was going to end it before I had said everything I wanted to. I was thoroughly into enjoying a dream come true! I looked at the blinking red light announcing my arrival into the world of comedy. I wish I could say "A Star is Born!" but it was more like "A New Hobby for Peter is Born!" Stand up comedy was just one more creative outlet for me to access as I learned how to express myself.

Photography was another outlet. I had done it since I was a child and picked up my first camera. Even then I was interested in having a creative outlet. As a boy, photography helped me create unique visions for myself and the world. The challenge was a little costly back then prior to digital photography so it remained mostly a dormant desire.

I leaned on my love for photography when my job took me from California to Hawaii. When I moved to Hawaii, my passion took off as I was fortunate to find an apartment in Waikiki with a great ocean view. I would take a photo of a sunset and put my camera down. A few minutes later, the sun would drop lower and create another beautiful image. This would continue at least three more times.

I also traveled around the islands and captured its native beauty that was displayed in beaches, waterfalls, and flowers. I photographed animals like sea turtles and roosters. Once I had amassed a wide collection of prints, I decided to display and sell them at the "Art Show on The Zoo Fence" in Waikiki which was held every weekend. It was usually a pleasant experience as Waikiki Beach was across the street, the zoo with all its animal sounds was behind us and trade winds created a gentle breeze.

It was enjoyable to meet people from all around the United States and the world. I made a game of trying to find common ground with as many people as possible. It was relatively easy with those from the U.S. as I had lived in seven states and had traveled to or through about 30 others. Among foreigners, I could relate an experience I had in the countries of Canada, Mexico, Iceland, Luxembourg, and France.

The vendor next to me was Chinese and spoke no English. I didn't know any Chinese. However, he was my banker. If it was early in the day and I needed change to give to a customer, I would just hand my neighbor a 20-dollar bill or whatever monetary unit I needed change for, and he would give me exactly what I needed.

I had a similar experience with a customer from Japan. I also did not speak Japanese and he didn't speak any English. However, I understood that he liked my photos of fireworks, so I traded him some of those for some photos he had taken of Mt. Fuji during different seasons. Our smiles communicated our gratification to each other.

Before I left my first Hawaiian employer, they asked me to perform stand-up comedy at the company Christmas party. The first rule of comedy is to know your audience so I needed to write a new routine that Hawaiians could relate to. I chose as my theme "Observations of Hawaiian Culture" and hoped that they wouldn't ask me to extinguish my flame and boot me off the island.

I talked about how drivers would flash a shaka (hand gesture meaning *hang loose*) at me when I let them go in front of me on the freeway and that I would struggle to respond in kind. I usually wound up flashing the *hook em horns* sign that the University of Texas uses.

Hawaiians refer to appetizers as Pu Pu's. They were delicious but the name said the opposite. I suggested that maybe that name was chosen because it was invented by some guy from Kaka'ako (an actual neighborhood in Honolulu). Finally, I took a very famous Hawaiian song, Henehene Kou 'Aka, and changed the lyrics. Below is the first verse:

Henehene Kou 'Aka
Wish I was Kama'aina
Things be mo' cheapah,
What could be mo' finah?

Andy Bumatai, a famous Hawaiian comic who was emceeing the open mic night where I appeared and told this joke, couldn't stop laughing when I finished and left the stage, so I guess it was okay.

After I moved to Hawaii, I decided I wanted to compete in the annual Toastmasters' International and Humorous speech competitions. The International competitions were mostly inspirational speeches, and the Humorous competitions were—wait for it—humorous speeches. I always had more fun writing and performing humorous speeches so that was my focus even though the winner of the international competition would get to compete wherever in the world it was held that year.

For my first humorous speech, I decided I needed to be more animated, so I created the setting of a zoo. I also wanted to pay tribute to Dr. Seuss, so the ending of every line rhymed with the "oo" sound. It went like this:

> Sitting at home (I pretended I was sitting on a chair); I didn't know what to do,
> And then it hit me (I smacked myself in the face and fell down), I know, I'll go to the zoo!

I won the first round and moved on to the second round. I won the second round and moved on to the final round competing against seven others from around the state of Hawaii. I received a lot of positive feedback and finished second! It was a fun experience.

For another humorous speech, I tried to imagine a situation that would be funny. I called it, "Public Speaking Tips," and I imitated Marlon Brando as the Godfather. If you haven't seen "*The Godfather*," he talks in a garbled fashion and not someone who sounds like he knows anything about public speaking.

"It's important when you speak to not sound like you have marbles in your mouth (which was exactly how I sounded), you want to enunciate (said with a slur), especially when you make an offer they can't refuse". Later I said that "You don't want to appear nervous when you speak and have your hands in your pockets. When I feel that way, I like to stroke my cat (this was the first scene from "The Godfather" and I had a stuffed cat). I know Toastmasters frowns on this sort of thing so let's lose the cat (which I threw across the stage). Don't worry, it has 9 lives." I didn't win but it made my day when the Japanese girl who won told me that she had never seen the movie but loved my speech!

A variety show was developed to celebrate when the Koreans first came to Hawaii. There were many different themes and events presented. I was given the opportunity to write and act in a production called "The Centurion." I wore fifty pounds of armor (and my back went out for two weeks after the event) portraying a centurion while delivering a five-minute soliloquy. It was just me and a hologram of Jesus on the cross. I started out mocking Him for not being able to save Himself and, by the end, asked for His forgiveness and to join Him in His Kingdom.

I currently live in a 55+ community in Florida. There are numerous clubs and activities that one could be involved in. One such club is the "Players Club." They put on theatrical productions. I decided to audition for a "Radio Readers Program." Three different radio programs were to be presented in front of a live audience. These were shows similar to the Fibber McGee and Molly programs in the 40s. I had a role in all three of them. My favorite was one in which I was a robot and spoke with a robot's voice throughout the show.

My performance was well-received and I was asked to audition for the Spring Play, "Murder For Dummies." I did and was given two roles: One as the "Book Voice" (I would be off-stage saying what the main character was reading in the book "Murder For Dummies") as well as the main character's neighbor describing what he was like to a reporter. I enjoyed the fact that both roles gave me the opportunity to make the audience laugh and I was successful in doing so.

MY FINAL THOUGHTS

It's difficult to describe the feeling when creativeness is flowing through my body with an overwhelming understanding that it's coming from another source. Often, I will look at the final product and say, "Wow! Where did that come from?!" I always know that it wasn't directly from me. It's such a great feeling to create something.

In retrospect, I believe the time I spent living inside myself during my high school years formed the foundation and development of my awareness of people's sensitivities to what they were experiencing, not just my own. Describing situations that others can relate to is the basis for successful writing whether it be comedic or serious.

Winning second place in the Hawaii Toastmasters competition reminded me how far I had come from dealing with a speech defect after contracting polio at the age of four.

NOW YOUR TURN

What creative talents do you have?

_____
_____
_____

Where do you find outlets to express them?

_____
_____
_____

Do you feel that your talent is strong enough for a career in that field?

_____
_____
_____

Do you feel God working through you when you're using your talent?

_____
_____
_____

CHAPTER TEN

FROSTBITTEN

COLD WEATHER HAS ALWAYS BEEN CHALLENGING TO ME. Despite the fact that I was born in Wisconsin, my body has never liked it. It didn't when I was growing up in Pennsylvania. It didn't when we moved to Michigan, especially on one particular Sunday morning when it was -40 degrees with the wind chill and I was a paperboy. I still had to deliver newspapers. And I delivered them faster than ever before that day.

I used to sing *California Dreamin* by the Mamas and Papas when I walked to high school in single digit temperatures, hoping that my mind over matter would block out how cold I was. I still wear sweat socks when I sleep because my toes were once frostbitten. Moving to New York when I transferred to another college and then New Jersey after I started my career didn't help either.

When I married my first wife in the Tri-State area, we decided to honeymoon in California to see what the land of "milk and honey" was all about. We flew to San Francisco and took two weeks to drive down the coast to San Diego. It was beautiful. We both decided we wanted to move there when the time was right. My wife was close to her grandmother and didn't want to leave while she was still alive. I also had just changed jobs and didn't think it would be right to leave so soon after that. Besides, I really liked the job and was learning a new skill.

We had a terrible snow storm one night in what was to be our last Winter on the East Coast. Six inches fell overnight. When I awoke, my car was completely covered in snow. I went out and brushed off the top and sides of my car. I went back inside, took a shower and dressed for work in a suit and tie.

However, when I came back out to go to work, I noticed that a snowplow had come by and pushed a ton of snow back up against my car. I went back inside and cried and was more determined than ever to move to a warmer climate.

Finally, the time had come to move to California. I went on a business trip to San Francisco and Los Angeles. I interviewed five companies located in one of those two cities. I told them that a job offer would need to include relocation expenses as I could not afford the move from the East Coast to the West Coast.

When I got back home, I received an offer from every company, and they all agreed to pay for our move. I decided to accept an offer from a company in Los Angeles because we liked the fact that it was warmer than San Francisco.

My wife loved her family and was really close to them. She wasn't looking forward to moving far away from them, so I went first to set things up and she joined me six weeks later. The minute she stepped off the plane, she started complaining that everything was better back East. This even included the beaches which I found hard to believe. To go to the "Shore" in the summer, we had to leave at 6:00 a.m., have breakfast once we arrived, then go to the beach and leave by 3:00 p.m. to avoid traffic heading back. It only took 30 minutes to go to the beach in Los Angeles and it was a lot less crowded.

There seemed to be constant tension between us from the very first day we got married. We couldn't leave our wedding reception and check in our hotel until we stopped at her parent's house first. This was because we needed to help them count and record the money they received from everyone. They needed to know this to make sure they gave at least as much money to other people's children if they got married.

Our honeymoon drive from San Francisco to San Diego reminded me of Charles Grodin and Jeannie Berlin in *The Heartbreak Kid* as they drove from New York to Miami. Our first argument concerned who gave us the better wedding gifts. My wife claimed that the gifts from her side were much better because they all gave us money whereas my family and friends from the Midwest gave us practical gifts. It didn't matter to me, but it did to my wife.

While the weather was warmer in California, our relationship started freezing over. Almost from the start, my wife wanted to move back East. We could never agree on that, so we eventually wound up in counseling. Our counselor came up with the idea that we would choose a city that we both could agree on and move there in two years if there was still unhappiness between us. My wife and I agreed on Atlanta. I am a huge Atlanta Braves fan plus it's warmer there than the East Coast. She liked it because it was a short flight to see her family.

The idea seemed to placate her until her family came for a visit. After they left, my wife said she changed her mind and she only wanted to move back home to be by her family. I suggested that she should go back there and live for a while and see what was more important to her, living on the East Coast or with me. She didn't want to do this, and things continued deteriorating between us until it got to the deep freeze level and I decided to leave.

MY FINAL THOUGHTS

My idea of utopia included warm weather and I was delighted to be moving to Southern California. However, I learned that it would take more than that to meet my criteria for happiness. For starters, it would include being in a warm-hearted, loving relationship.

Red flags at the beginning of a honeymoon are a terrible omen. It usually can only get worse. My theory is that it is difficult not to marry the first person you think you're in love with because you don't know any better. You have nothing to compare it to. To be happy in a committed, married relationship requires being divorced from your family to a certain degree. Overall, I believe that someone's idea of utopia is formed over time after encountering both positive and negative experiences.

NOW YOUR TURN

Do you live in a part of the country where the weather is really cold and there is a lot of snow in the Winter?

_____
_____
_____

If so, do you desire to move elsewhere to a warmer climate?

_____
_____
_____

What might be keeping you from doing that if that is your desire?

_____
_____
_____

Are you in a relationship that has turned cold?

_____
_____
_____

If so, what can you do to turn the heat back up in it?

_____
_____
_____

CHAPTER ELEVEN

CHANGING DIRECTIONS

My life changed when I moved West to California from the East Coast, and then again when I got divorced. I met a woman several years later and remarried and shortly after became a father. Both those experiences changed my life and put me down new paths.

My first daughter, Melissa, was born in California. I was so excited on the day that she was born that I went home and listened to and sang "*Sweet Melissa*" by the Allman Brothers repeatedly!

It was such a delight watching Melissa grow and literally reach new heights. She climbed out of her crib at six months, climbed baseball backstops at two and at three, climbed door jambs. She excelled in gymnastics, dancing and then figure skating at the age of ten. She was the only skater who fell in her first competition but won the event easily. Her determination was, and is, her greatest strength and she has used it to overachieve throughout her life.

Jessica came about four years later. If you recall, "*Jessica*" was the theme song for Radio Monte Carlo when the station came on at 6 PM every night in France. Little did the Allman Brothers know that they were naming my daughters when they wrote "*Sweet Melissa*" and "*Jessica*." Again, I was so excited when Jessica was born that I went home and listened to the song repeatedly. It was a jazzy instrumental tune that lasted nearly eight minutes. I'd just hum along with it, so excited about my brand new baby girl.

Jessica had a quieter demeanor than Melissa and a much more introspective nature about her. I also noticed that when I would pick her up from grade school, she was surrounded by numerous children. Given her quiet nature, this seemed unusual. Being curious, I asked one of her teachers what she thought the attraction was and she simply said, "Jessica has a great deal of integrity, and other children respond positively to it."

While Melissa's prowess grew as she got older, in Jessica's case, it was her intelligence and intellect that blossomed. Both girls have a caring nature about them, and I couldn't be prouder that they're my daughters.

Every year around Thanksgiving, my daughters would ask if we were going to have a "White Christmas" as they wanted to experience snow, especially at that time of year. Of course, my answer always disappointed them. So, I decided that we would go visit my sister and her family in Rochester, Minnesota during February.

It always snowed there at this time so I knew my daughters would finally have the experience they were seeking. One of the activities that I enjoyed as a child when it snowed was building a snowman. There was something magical about creating a person out of snow. That was our first goal when we arrived.

However, snow can vary from being soft and fluffy to wet and easy to make snowballs with it. The snow at my sister's house was the first type so it was impossible to build a snowman. We kept driving around to other areas in town hoping for better results. We finally found some snow that was serviceable, and we were moderately successful in our task.

My favorite snow activity when I was younger was sledding down steep hills. This was the next activity on our list. We found the perfect hill and I watched as my daughters gleefully sled down each time. Jessica was around five at this time and was very lightweight. She went down in a circular sled which I never liked because it was difficult to steer. Suddenly, I noticed that she was catching up to an older man on a wooden sled. I watched in horror as her sled caught up to him and she flew in the air! I could barely breathe as I watched her do a somersault in midair and then land squarely back down on her sled and continued down the hill, totally unharmed.

I asked her later if she recalled what happened and how she was able to do what she did. She replied that her friend Sally helped her, and that Sally had also helped her on other occasions. I had a sister named Sally who was really close to my brother Allen who had passed away not long before that. I don't know if this was the connection that saved my daughter, but I do know that someone up there was watching out for her.

I enjoyed the change in direction from the East Coast to the West Coast. Life was freer and easier. There was a certain warmth about everything, including the people. New York and its residents seemed to be a lot more uptight about things.

Before moving to California, I had to go into the New York office of the company that hired me for some training. One night, while I was waiting for the train to take me home, I started talking to a total stranger standing next to me. When I mentioned that I was moving to Los Angeles, he said, "Well, you can take L.A. and shove it up your ass for all I care!" I found it interesting that New Yorkers don't like people in Los Angeles, but Angelenos couldn't care less about New Yorkers. They're too busy enjoying life.

When I lived in the Los Angeles area, San Francisco was always referred to as "Northern California." Having driven the length of the state on my way to Seattle, I soon realized that it is just a little north of "Central California." It takes eight hours to drive from San Diego to San Francisco and another six-and-a-half hours to go from there to Oregon.

Every state in the United States is like its own little country with all the towns and areas in it having a myriad of history, culture, geography, etc. Because of its size, California has a lot more of this than other states and it seems like it would take a lifetime to discover everything it has. I lived there for 25 years and welcomed every opportunity to learn whatever insights I could find.

When I first arrived in California, it was like being on vacation all the time compared to New Jersey. I asked locals where they go and they all said, "Hawaii!" I tucked that thought in the back of my brain, determined to visit there someday. However, I never did for the 25 years I lived there until I had to go there for a job interview. Once I landed the job, it was time to bid Aloha to California and Aloha to Hawaii.

When I first arrived at the airport in Honolulu, I was greeted with a lei by an airport employee who told me that I could never get lost "because it's an island and you'll just drive around in circles until you find where you're going." Little did I know that this would be an apt description of my time in Hawaii.

Shortly after I arrived, I kept thinking "Why am I here?" Sure, I was living in "paradise" on the 24th floor of a high-rise in Waikiki overlooking the ocean with great sunset views, driving a BMW and earning more money than I had ever made before. But it felt like something was missing. I would ponder that question repeatedly whenever I walked around Waikiki, ran along the Ala Wai Canal or drove around the island.

A few months after I arrived, I developed a case of hives. This only added to the mystery. There were just a few at first but they gradually spread all over my body during a six-week period. I was constantly putting cream on them to keep them from itching.

I saw my regular doctor who put me on a special diet to see if I was allergic to food. That didn't work. I saw an allergist who stuck 40 needles in my back to try and determine the cause. That didn't work either. I even moved a Persian rug that I had recently bought out onto my lanai with the same results.

Then, one night, as I was watching TV, I felt one forming near my eye. I knew if I didn't do something that I would be blind in that eye in the morning, so I went to the ER. They intravenously injected me with Benadryl and steroids. That finally cured me, and the hives went away. No more diet and the rug was returned to the living room. I looked at the hives and the simplicity of its cure as a metaphor for how to adjust to my new surroundings.

Since I had never been to Hawaii before, I felt and acted like a tourist. Not only did I try to see as many of the sights on the island as possible, but I also bought numerous souvenir items like prints for my walls, mugs, bowls, T-shirts and, of course, a whole new wardrobe of aloha shirts.

Since Hawaii had no professional sports teams, I would go to University of Hawaii (UH) football, basketball and baseball games. It was big news anytime one of our players made it to the majors, like Kolten Wong, who played in the Major League for more than ten years, mostly with the St. Louis Cardinals. My company had tickets to see UH football games and my friend Bob and I would use them as much as possible. It was exciting as they went undefeated one year (only to get crushed by Georgia in a bowl game).

Bob was also new to the island, and we bonded and would often tell each other that we hoped we would last on the island at least three years and no one would come and tell us to extinguish our torch before then.

One year, a friend asked me to join her at a "Son Rise" service on Easter. I'm not really a morning person and the thought of getting up before the sun is out doesn't really appeal to me. However, I do like experiencing different adventures, so I did, and we arrived in pitch-black darkness and watched the sun rise as the worship service began. It was a lovely service with great worship music, hula dancers and a profound message by the Pastor.

It certainly moved me and, at the end of the service when the Pastor asked if anyone in the audience would like Jesus in their life, I raised my hand. I was stunned to see that no one else raised their hand. Later, I realized that it was because they already had Jesus in their life. I met with the Pastor afterwards and he explained what I was committing to and that I would be receiving the free gift of salvation.

I repeated this prayer after him:

> "Dear Lord Jesus, I know that I am a sinner, and I ask for Your forgiveness. I believe You died for my sins and rose from the dead. I turn from my sins and invite You to come into my heart and life. I want to trust and follow You as my Lord and Savior. In Your Name. Amen."

This commitment definitely provided a new direction in my life. I no longer believed that I was accomplishing everything on my own. I realized I had a Friend walking beside me who had been there from the beginning. He was there when I overcame polio. He was there protecting me in all my life-or-death situations. He provided me with my creative talents. Every time I found myself in the wrong place at the wrong time in my career, He provided me with an even better opportunity.

I met "Uncle Jay" at an elders meeting for my church. He had founded Common Grace after a study of the Columbine tragedy found that likely shooters were students who were quiet, lonely, lacked friends and were socially rejected and bullied. His concept was to have adults mentor students that fit in this category. Interestingly, it was adults from Christian churches mentoring students from public schools.

His recipe for "Goodness" was known as C.A.K.E. and included:

- Compassion—connecting and understanding elementary school children on an emotional level;
- Attention—providing an undivided focus on a child;
- Kindness—giving of oneself towards a child without expecting anything in return; and
- Encouragement—providing positive reinforcement to instill courage and confidence in a child.

Mentors would meet with students for one hour one day a week. The time would be broken up into segments that included talking to the student and seeing how they were doing, helping with homework and playing games.

Since I was the program coordinator for my church, along with input from school counselors, I matched the students with the mentors. I chose Dennis for my student. We had some common ground in that we both had lived near Philadelphia, liked sports, especially football and baseball and playing games like hangman, tic tac toe and four in a row.

The counselors had told me that Dennis would often just sit in the counselors' room and not talk to anyone. It was difficult to get him out of his shell. Dennis also reminded me of myself as I grew up quiet and shy. I saw my goal as helping Dennis reach his full potential as a person and escaping his self-imposed prison of a shell.

At first, he didn't say much but he gradually started talking more. He loved playing games and that seemed to be the bridge to connect with him. He also enjoyed talking about sports whether it be about the Philadelphia Eagles or Phillies or even the University of Hawaii (UH) sports teams. I made it a point to get to know his family as well. His Dad had tickets to UH sports events and I would often be invited to join them.

I encouraged other mentors to get to know their students' families too. We had an annual event each Spring and invited family members to join in the fun. One of my favorite meetings with Dennis was seeing him on the day after Christmas each year and playing some of his new games with him, especially Madden Football. The mentorships lasted from first grade through fifth grade.

I stayed in contact with Dennis through eighth grade and enjoyed watching him mature into a well-developed individual. I also went to see him play football, basketball and baseball and was impressed with his talent and could see how sports had helped him grow. When Dennis entered high school, the Common Grace program had expanded to include students at that level mentoring elementary school students. It gave me great joy when I heard that Dennis' life had gone full circle, and he was now mentoring a student!

When I moved from California to Hawaii, I was separated from my second wife. Melissa was about to enter 12th grade and Jessica, 8th grade. It was extremely difficult telling them that I was moving to Hawaii. It was one of the hardest things I have ever had to do. I knew it wouldn't register at the time, but I told them that they could come visit me in Hawaii. I thought it might improve their mood a little. It didn't.

The girls did come to visit me a few times and, a few years after I arrived, Melissa called me and told me she wanted to come and live with me. I was so excited about re-establishing our father-daughter relationship after living apart for a few years. She lived with me for three years until she moved to Kansas with her fiancé who got transferred to a military base there.

Shortly after Melissa moved out, I received a call from Jessica who said she also wanted to come live with me. She, too, stayed with me for three years until she decided she wanted to see the world at age 25 and moved to Australia with her boyfriend. Twenty-five was the same age that I was when I first went to France so I understood and believed she should see the world while she was still young.

MY FINAL THOUGHTS

When I was in my 20s, I never thought I would get married. Later, when I changed my mind about that, I didn't think I wanted to have any children. Somehow, life takes you by the hand and, sometimes, leads you down a road you didn't think you would ever go down. Utopia finds you when you are not searching for it.

My experience in California reinforced my desire to live in a generally warm climate. I also learned that lifestyle was just as important for my sense of utopia. Hawaii has the best climate that I have ever experienced but living on an island has its limitations in terms of cost of living expenses, job opportunities, restaurant choices, activities and travel.

I found that I really enjoyed mentoring children, especially those that I could relate to. I know what I went through growing up and it gives me pleasure to try and help them overcome hurdles and develop their personalities and attributes. It gives me great satisfaction knowing that Dennis, the student that I mentored, has graduated from college and is now on the Board of Directors for Common Grace.

It is important to maintain strong relationships with your children, even when and especially when you live apart. Don't let time and distance get in the way of this. I love it when my daughters contact me for advice. I even enjoy playing "Words With Friends" with Melissa as I feel like I'm communicating with her when I do. Jessica and I share photos with each other so we each can see what's going on in each other's life.

NOW YOUR TURN

Have you ever experienced a change in direction in your life? Was it intentional or unintentional or have you experienced both?

_____
_____
_____

Were the results of the change as anticipated?

_____
_____
_____

Would you do anything differently?

_____
_____
_____

What have you learned from the experience?

_____
_____
_____

CHAPTER TWELVE

DELAYERING

WHEN I MADE THE DECISION TO LEAVE HOLLYWOOD and go back to the business world, my goal was to land a job in risk management. I eventually succeeded when I got an opportunity to work as a Risk Manager with a large defense contractor. My hope was to use both my technical and creative abilities to devise creative financial approaches in lieu of buying insurance.

Unfortunately, since the company worked on government contracts, we were not allowed to stray from buying traditional insurance products. Therefore, when a 1,000-store retailer asked me to be their first Risk Manager, I leapt at the opportunity.

Initially, I used my creative talent to develop risk management processes, programs and procedures. I worked closely with the Legal Department in reviewing insurance language in contracts, devising insurance requirements for vendors and contractors and providing input on claims. My favorite responsibility was working closely with our insurance broker to develop alternative risk funding mechanisms.

This lasted two years until the day I heard a word that I had never heard before, even though I had a broad vocabulary. That is never a good thing. The company was struggling financially, and they hired a new CFO to try and turn things around. One day, he called me into his office. He started the conversation by saying that the company was going through a "delayering" process. This sounded ominous. My comedic brain wanted me to say something like, "So, does this mean that all of the employees get to share a piece of layer cake to celebrate the company's success?"

The mature side of my brain squashed that idea and played it straight. When I questioned what it meant, his response was that the company was eliminating the risk management position. I verbalized my first reaction by asking who in the company was going to take over that responsibility. I was aghast when he told me that the Human Resources Director would now handle it. She had no insurance or risk management experience. However, the company soon folded after that, so it was irrelevant.

For my next job, I decided to work as an Underwriter handling large risk management accounts for one of the largest insurance companies. I would use my risk manager connections to solicit business, my actuarial background to develop premiums for the insurance product and my creative ability to design the product. Over the years, I realized that I work best when I can use as many of my talents as possible and this fits that mold.

As time went on, my personality became more outgoing, and I became more interested in marketing. The head of Marketing in our New York home office told me about a marketing manager opportunity in the San Francisco office. I always enjoyed going to that city and thought it would be a great way to further my career growth. I decided to take the professional route and tell our office manager my interest. He said he would talk to the people involved about me.

Months went by without me hearing anything further about it. Finally, the head of Marketing told me that my office manager blackballed me. Sure enough, when I had my annual review with the office manager and my supervisor, they told me that they "only wanted people to work there who wanted to work in Los Angeles." I was stunned and felt betrayed. I received the lowest rating on my review in every category offered. It felt like my career was being flushed down the toilet! What saved me was that the former office manager had left to work for a competitor and was interested in my talents. I escaped before getting axed and went to work as a Marketing Representative, exactly the area where I now wanted to focus my talents. A few years later, I ran into my former office manager at an insurance conference. He apologized to me for how he had treated me. Although, my next job was much better for me, I still appreciated his apology. It meant a lot to me.

My next role allowed me to use my marketing skills as well as my underwriting ability. The goal was to solicit large risk management accounts from major insurance brokers. Having worked in the industry for a while, I knew quite a few of these brokers as well as the risk managers for the companies that we wanted to insure.

However, after a year there, the company changed course and decided to go after "program business." Instead of looking to insure single entities, we wanted to insure groups of similar insureds. This meant that we had a different production source. Instead of large brokers, we now needed to solicit business from consultants and regional brokers. The company also wanted us to improve our "hit ratio" by being more discriminating in the accounts we went after.

Despite having to start from scratch, I established relationships with new production sources and had an extremely profitable year. I met my production goal while writing a large percentage of the accounts that I quoted. I couldn't wait until March when we would receive our bonuses. However, the company's Chairman of the Board, a former banker, decided that he wasn't getting a quick enough return on his investment, so he decided to eliminate the risk management division that I worked in.

Instead of a monetary reward, we all got pink slips. It caught me off guard. I was so surprised because I worked with amazing people who were All-Stars in the insurance industry.

Earlier in the year, my brother moved his family from Georgia back to Michigan so they could be near his dying father-in-law. When he passed away, I called my brother to try and console him. There was a popular Bud Lite beer commercial at the time where one man tells another, "I love you man" in hopes that the other man will give him his Bud Lite. The other man always replied, "I love you man, too, but you're still not getting my Bud Lite." In trying to cheer my brother up, my last words to him were, "I love you man" and he responded by saying "I love you too but you're still not getting my Bud Lite."

Two weeks later my brother died.

One of the girls who worked for him at a country club came to the funeral. I wanted some way to remember my brother, so I asked her what his favorite song was. She said it was "Tequila" because my brother said that there weren't a lot of words to remember.

After the funeral, I got in my sister's car and "Tequila" was playing on the radio!

After a stream of job changes, layoffs, and cuts, I found myself in a deep depression. After being laid off from the insurance company, I had a hard time with life. To make matters worse, my personal life had really fallen apart right around the same time. After my brother died, I decided to take a trial separation period from my wife at the time. This was turning into the toughest year of my life. The challenge to move forward was daunting.

When one of the consultants that I had a relationship with heard about what happened with my job, he called and asked if I had ever tried consulting. I said I hadn't, and he offered me the opportunity to work for him. I would work out of his home office, an hour and half away, and only get paid commission but I didn't know what else to do so I accepted it. I also needed something else to focus on after losing my only brother.

I worked for him for about a year and did well. However, the commute was draining. I eventually wanted to buy a house for my family, so I accepted a different position as a Senior Consultant with a risk management consulting company. Unfortunately, it was also an hour and a half away. My wife and I were back together and since I was getting a salary again with the new risk management consulting company, I was able to buy a house closer to work and eliminate my commute.

Most of the work I did in my new role was risk management audits of both public and private entities. The first one was for a large county in Washington state. Most of the others were cities in California. I also did one for a large RV manufacturer. Years earlier when the company was a lot smaller, they chose a small, regional broker to handle their insurance. The company's CFO already had an established relationship with the broker who would be handling their account. Now that the manufacturer had grown a lot larger, it seemed like they outgrew the available resources of their current broker so I suggested that they go through a "broker selection" process where they would consider the opportunity to work with a different, and possibly, larger broker. That is exactly what the company decided to do.

Shortly after the switch to a larger broker, I was invited to lunch by the Sales Manager for the new broker. He wanted to get my feedback about what they did well and what they could improve on. At lunch, the broker told me that they help people get risk manager positions in case I was interested in doing that again. I told him I wasn't at that time, and he asked what interested me the most. I told him I enjoyed working with public entities and bells went off in his head. That was an area where his firm was lacking so I was offered a position as a Vice President and Public Entity Practice Leader.

My role was to handle and place business on large risk management accounts as well as work with Sales professionals in obtaining public entity business. I also performed captive feasibility studies and trained staff on performing cash flow analyses. I thrived in this new role for three years and then…it happened again! Our company got nailed by the attorney general of New York for committing fraudulent activities in our New York office. We had to pay hundreds of millions of dollars in fines and started having massive layoffs. Our 401k was all in company stock which was worth nothing! I immediately started looking for another opportunity before I was let go.

I looked everywhere in the Southern California area for my next job. Then I looked in Northern California around San Francisco. I also checked out Phoenix, Arizona. I couldn't find anything in any of these places. Then, a friend of mine who worked for our company in our Hawaii office sent me an ad seeking someone to work in Honolulu.

The position was Vice President – Pricing and Rate Filing. The requirements read like my resume. They needed someone with experience in actuarial, programs, reinsurance and captives. I applied and was asked to go there for interviews over a three-day period. I was told to leave my business suits at home and to bring aloha/Hawaiian shirts. I didn't own any, so I quickly went to the mall and picked out two that weren't too outlandish.

I had a series of interviews over the first two days. I wasn't used to wearing an aloha shirt during job interviews, so I didn't have my usual confidence. I felt like a clown. While I was being interviewed by one of the executives, I looked out his window and saw a rainbow. I was amazed and thought it was a good sign. The interviewer dismissed it with a remark of "Oh, we get those all the time here." Maybe so, but I was delighted to witness it at that time.

I had free time on the third day, so I decided to rent a car and drive around the island while seeing as many sights as possible and getting a taste of island life in case I was offered the job. When I returned home, I received a call offering me the job. Since I had no other options, I accepted it and said "Aloha California, Aloha Hawaii."

My new job came with a salary far more than the most I had made previously, along with a yearly company bonus. However, the dream turned into a nightmare as my boss, the President, decided he didn't like how I did things. I thought that with all the money he had invested in bringing me to Hawaii, he would have taken the time to train me in his methods but, instead, he tried to convince me to leave by lowering my salary by $50,000.

I learned later that this was his modus operandi – hiring employees from the mainland but discarding them soon thereafter if they didn't live up to his standards. I soon learned that living on an island has many limitations – one of them being a lack of well-paying opportunities.

My employer didn't like to fire people so he kept hoping, as I did, that I would leave. Finally, he let me go along with a severance package. He gave that to me on a Friday. Little did he know that I was to start my new job on Monday with a family-owned insurance brokerage firm!

The cycle continued yet again as my new employer had financial difficulties and had to let me go after eight months. It took another six months, but I found a job as a Sales Rep for a national insurance company. I received the call on my birthday and was excited that I would get to travel to all the islands to meet with clients and prospects.

This lasted for two years until the company decided to change the way they did business after 100 years. No longer were they soliciting business directly from potential clients. Instead, they were going to do it the traditional way of working with brokers to get opportunities. This meant that they no longer needed Sales Reps and no longer needed my services. Once again, I was able to overcome this challenge by meeting a person who had also worked for the same company but now had his own insurance agency. He needed another employee, and I needed a job, so it became a reality.

It was a commission-only position, so I supplemented my income at first by selling prints of my photos of sunsets, beaches, flowers, etc. at a local art show on the weekends. As I described earlier, our art was hung on a fence outside the Honolulu Zoo. Later, I sold furniture imported from Indonesia out of a storage facility. Finally, a national hardware store opened, and I got a part-time job with them selling appliances. I had to be able to work all shifts and will never forget driving home at 2 a.m. one morning and saying to myself, "I can't believe I'm 60 years old and working 60 hours a week."

This lasted nine months until I was saved by the largest insurance broker in Hawaii buying the agency I worked for. This meant I would get a salary and not have to work at the hardware store anymore. My back, knees and ankles were sore from standing on concrete for eight hours at a time. Also, the Christmas holidays were coming, and I knew that they would expect me to work a lot of hours during that period. At last, I had employment stability as this next job lasted six and a half years, the longest tenure in my career.

MY FINAL THOUGHTS

Prior to the 1980's, it was not unusual for someone to spend their entire career with one company. Once the mergers and acquisitions craze started, this became a rarity. To survive during this period, one needed to redefine themselves. The more skills you possess, the broader the range of job opportunities for you.

My father used to tell me that I could do anything I wanted to if I just put my mind to it. He was right and I did just that each time I needed to find a new job. Whenever I found myself in the wrong place at the wrong time, the next job was always better than the last one. My faith in being able to do this kept growing each time it happened. After I became a Christian in 2006, my faith in God and His plan for me further solidified my resolve. Each time I needed to find new employment, I would hear God tell me, "Well, you said you needed challenges." Be careful what you wish for.

Losing my brother at such a young age was much worse than losing any job I ever had. Losing so much at the same time gave me plenty of opportunities for prayer and turning to God. Rather than remember the day my brother died, I celebrate the day he was born. Every year on my brother's birthday, I go to a Mexican restaurant and order a shot of tequila and a Bud Lite chaser. I raise the glass of tequila and yell "Tequila!" and chase it with the Bud Lite and toast my brother and say, "I love you man!"

NOW YOUR TURN

Have you ever been in the "wrong place at the wrong time" and lost your job?

_____
_____

How did you react to losing it?

_____
_____

Was your next job better than the one you lost?

_____
_____

What did you learn from the experience?

_____
_____

If, and when, you lose a job, do you always have faith that you will be able to find another one?

_____
_____

CHAPTER THIRTEEN
LOVE, AT LAST

I T WAS MY 63RD BIRTHDAY. A WOMAN THAT I HAD BEEN SEEing for five years celebrated with me over a picnic lunch. I couldn't imagine a better way to celebrate my birthday than with a picnic in Hawaii!

Lunch was lovely. It was really more like two friends celebrating my birthday than two lovers. After that day, I realized our relationship had descended to a "friendship" level, and it was time to move on. Each of us had evolved since we first met and both of us were wiser about who we were and what we wanted in a partner. That person was still somewhere out there, wherever "there" was and "she" was.

At my age and stage in life, it was difficult to meet someone who I might be interested in. I couldn't date anyone from my job or any of my clients. I wasn't interested in anyone from my church. I didn't hang out in bars, nor did I belong to any clubs. While I preferred a more natural process, I opted to try online dating.

The process involved seeing someone online who I might be interested in based on her photo and her self-description of who she was and what she was looking for in a partner. Then, I would communicate by email or phone and, if there is still an interest, we would eventually meet after some light-hearted chatting.

That's the tricky part. I would get excited about the possibility of meeting someone who seemed to be a good match for me and hope that there will be a "connection" when we finally did meet. In my case, I never felt a connection once I met someone who had interested me via online dating. It got to be redundant saying "I think we're better off as friends." I said it time and time again over the course of a year. And then…

I have a love of theater. It started when I acted in my high school's Senior Play. Later, I wrote, produced and directed a One-Act play while still in high school. When I attended college in New York City, I took an elective class where we went to see a different production every week. This included Broadway, off-Broadway and Shakespeare In The Park.

Honolulu had a local theater called Diamond Head Theatre. They were going to present a production of White Christmas and one of my friends had a lead role in it. So, without knowing whom I would be going with, I purchased two tickets. At that time, I had met a few women online and thought that at least one of them would be available. The first woman I asked lived three blocks from me in Waikiki. She wanted to go but was leaving that day for Oregon to spend the holidays with her son. So, I asked Nancy, a woman I had gone out with a few times. I didn't think the relationship would develop into more than a friendship but thought it would still be fun to see the show together. She agreed but wanted to meet at the theater instead of me picking her up.

I was standing by the drink cart outside the Diamond Head Theatre checking out the options. Nancy had not arrived yet and I got there early to get our tickets from the box office. I heard a woman say, "I'm not sure what I want."

I turned to see who made the comment and was immediately struck by the beauty of the woman standing next to me, especially her eyes. Keeping with the season, she was dressed in a very sexy red dress. Being a gentleman, I made a point of only looking at her from the chin up.

Conversation flowed freely and I was really taken by her. However, the more we talked, the more anxious I became because I knew Nancy would show up at any minute. Even though we weren't seriously dating, I wanted to be sensitive to her feelings.

I learned that the woman I was talking to was named Monica. She had three jobs, and one was as a tram driver at Hanauma Bay, a popular snorkeling area on Oahu. I didn't want to be too aggressive, so I didn't ask her for her phone number. Finally, I said that I was waiting for a "friend." Using her woman's intuition, she said it was okay, but could we still talk until "she" got here? My emotion trumped my intellect and I said "Yes."

It wasn't long before I saw Nancy standing on the sidewalk 20 yards away. I told Monica I had to leave and that I enjoyed meeting her. She echoed my sentiment and went inside, and I went to greet Nancy.

The first thing Nancy said was, "I thought I came on the wrong night" (again, women's intuition"). I told her she hadn't, and that Monica was just someone I was talking to at the drink cart while trying to decide what to get later. We went inside and watched the show. I kept wishing I was sitting next to Monica instead of Nancy.

After the show, we waited outside so I could say hello to my actress friend. I caught a glimpse of Monica leaving and suppressed a smile. Nancy and I went our separate ways and when I got to my car, I wrote down "Monica, tram operator,

Hanauma Bay" so that I wouldn't forget about her. I put her name on my refrigerator so it was something I saw often. I didn't call her right away because it was the Christmas season which is not always an easy time to start a relationship.

One morning a month later, I woke up and the first thing I heard was a voice that said, "Call Monica!"

I thought to myself, "I can do that." The only problem was that I did not have her phone number. However, I did remember that one of her jobs was driving a tram up and down a steep hill for visitors at Hanauma Bay, a popular snorkeling site.

I called Hanauma Bay, but they said I needed to contact the tram company and gave me that number. I called the tram company and got Monica's boss. She wouldn't give me Monica's number but took mine to give to her. I was out when Monica called but she left her number, and I called her back. I said, "Hi, I don't know if you remember me, but this is Peter, we met outside Diamond Head Theatre last month". She said, "Of course I remember you; you have the prettiest blue eyes I've ever seen and what took you so long to call me?!" I loved her initiative and was immediately hooked.

Our first date was at a wine bar. I asked her what her favorite wine was, and she said, "white wine" and referred to it as "cooking wine."

Since she hadn't experienced red wine before, I introduced her to wines like Cabernet Sauvignon and Pinot Noir. The conversation flowed freely like the first time we met until she asked me how old I was. Most people think I look younger than I am, so I asked her how old she thought I was. She said she didn't know and repeated the question. I told her my age—15 years older than her—and hoped that her approach to life was the same as mine—age is as irrelevant as ears on an elephant.

I thought if she just gave me a chance, she would find it to be true and we could be good for each other.

I learned on our first date that Monica was unable to attend church on Sundays because she worked on those days. My church had a Friday night service, so I invited her to attend with me, which is where we went on our second date. I was happy that she was a fellow Christian but felt a little uncomfortable sitting in the front. I usually sat in the back, but she liked to sit up front so that the choir could drown her out if she was off key. This was the beginning of Monica challenging my comfort level and causing me to personally grow. We went to dinner after the service and the conversation flowed freely again. It seemed like we were off to a good start and there was a possibility that we could overcome the age difference.

Usually, when two people meet and are attracted to each other, they initially spend time "doing social things together." This would include going to dinner, movies, concerts, etc. The time is spent enjoying activities while getting to know each other better. However, this doesn't represent real life or how couples normally spend their time together.

Since Monica was in the process of moving, we spent time together doing more mundane things. I helped her organize and pack boxes. She was also selling a lot of furniture and other household items. With my sales background, I helped her with that and "upsold" to willing buyers.

Eventually, Monica joined me on business trips to the other islands. First, it was Kona on the Big Island. After indulging in room service pizza, we went to a local bar where our first dance together was to "Shut up and Dance" by Walk The Moon. I was literally moonstruck the entire evening!

On another trip, we went to the island of Molokai, where lepers used to be exiled. My client there reinstated the island's annual rodeo. This was the first rodeo I ever attended, and I thoroughly enjoyed it. Prior to this trip, I never really liked country music. However, that's all the radio stations played while we were there. Not only did I begin to like it, but I got up in the middle of the night to write a country song, "This Ain't Our First Rodeo, Girl."

We were supposed to fly back to Honolulu the next day at 7:00 p.m. However, the plane from there couldn't land on Molokai because of the weather conditions so the flight was canceled until the next day. The airport was closing at 11:00 p.m.and we had already given up the condo we rented and turned in the car rental. We had nowhere to go but to sleep on the sidewalk outside the airport.

Most women I know would have freaked out. However, Monica had met a woman who lived on Molokai and offered her a place for us to stay that night. The woman also made us breakfast in the morning and drove us back to the airport. It's really true that Molokai is known as "The Friendly Isle."

We had another delightful trip to Kauai where we celebrated my birthday. Kauai is the least developed island and still possesses a lot of its natural beauty. It even has a "mini–Grand Canyon", Waimea Canyon. Many movies were filmed here like "South Pacific" on the Na Pali Coast.

However, it was a little nerve-wracking driving around the island as the speed limit kept changing and it seemed like there was a police car on the corner whenever it was lowered. It would go from 45 to 35 to 25 to 35 to 25 to 45 to 35, etc. I had a headache after only driving for 30 minutes under these conditions. Overall, though, it was another wonderful time traveling and exploring Hawaii and getting to know each other.

Another memorable trip was to Maui where we celebrated Monica's birthday. We enjoyed dinner at a great Italian restaurant in Lahaina called "Longhi's", which unfortunately was burned down during the wildfires there. We also went to Surfing Goat Dairy which raised goats and made 20 different types of goat and feta cheese. Their motto is "Our Feta is Mo' Bettah!" and it is. We sampled numerous cheeses and bought some to eat while sampling wine nearby at the Maui Winery. Later, we toured Ali'I Kula Lavender, a lavender farm with endless rows of 45 varieties of the flower overlooking the ocean. It also has a gift shop with lavender infused products.

As time went on, I realized that I liked Monica's caring and loving personality. She also had a great sense of humor which is a necessity for anyone living with me. We shared Christian values, love of family and a desire to see the world. We enjoyed going to the theater and had season tickets. It seemed like we were meant for each other. Having been married before, I didn't want to choose poorly again but I easily envisioned a life together with Monica.

I enjoyed preparing and giving Toastmasters speeches. I was looking for an alternative to insurance/risk management for when I retired and decided that public speaking was the answer. Normally, Toastmaster speeches are seven minutes long. However, speeches for the Professional Speaker projects needed to be 20 minutes long and I needed to create a "brand" for public speaking. The brand I chose, which was also the title of my speech, was "You're Never Too Old."

I was scheduled to present my speech at the meeting on March 17th, St. Patrick's Day. Monica worked as a school nurse and there was no school on that day, so I invited her to hear my speech. She gladly accepted. In my speech, I shared things that I accomplished after the age of 50. This included becoming a stand-up comedian at the age of 52, a photographer at 55 and winning 2nd place in the state of Hawaii's Toastmasters

Humorous Speech competition at 62. I then proceeded to share how I fell in love at 64.

I mentioned how, in the past, I made the mistake of falling for a woman's beauty but didn't take the time to see what her personality was like. This time, I wanted to be sure that I wasn't just settling for someone. I was enamored with Monica's personality and showed photos that exemplified it like riding in a shopping cart, climbing a tree by a sign that said, "Do Not Climb On The Tree" and dropping off goods at the back of a thrift store where the sign, of course, said, "Do Not Drop Off Goods." I could very easily see Monica becoming my "partner in crime."

At this point in the speech, I mentioned that my fellow Toastmasters had met Monica via the photos I had shown but now I wanted them to meet her in person, so I invited her to come join me. When she did, I said, "Fellow Toastmasters, this is Monica. Monica, these are my fellow Toastmasters and, one other thing, will you marry me?" After a brief giggle, she said yes!

MY FINAL THOUGHTS

Meeting Monica was divine intervention. Originally, I was going to go to the theater with another woman who lived three blocks from me. However, she changed her plans because she was leaving for Oregon on the day of the show to be with her son for the holidays. If she had gone with me, we would have gone together, and I wouldn't have met Monica.

On the other hand, Monica usually went on another night with lady friends but was unable to, so she went on the night we met instead. When I heard the voice that said to call her that morning, I knew it was a "Godwink" and pre-planned. I had prayed to meet a nice Christian woman. Monica had prayed to meet someone she wouldn't have to drag to church and was 6 feet tall with blue eyes. Both our prayers were answered.

I had learned from prior marriages the importance of personality in a potential partner. She had to be as beautiful on the inside as she was on the outside. I also knew that it was important that we enjoyed each other's company when we were together, even if we weren't doing anything special. Finally, since I liked to travel so much, it was necessary that she had the same spirit of adventure, and our trips together were enjoyable. When Monica checked all these boxes, I knew I had been blessed with a potential lifetime partner.

NOW YOUR TURN

Have you found yourself without a partner late in life (after age 50)?

_____
_____
_____
_____

Have you given up hope of meeting someone special again?

_____
_____
_____
_____

Is your heart open to meeting someone again?

_____
_____
_____
_____

What is your mindset now that you find yourself in this situation?

_____
_____
_____
_____

CHAPTER FOURTEEN

WEDDING AND HONEYMOON

When I asked Monica where she wanted to get married, she immediately replied, "In front of the Eiffel Tower!" Since we lived in Hawaii, which was a popular destination for weddings, it made sense to me that we would choose another locale. It had been 42 years since I had been in Paris and missed out on seeing Monet's wall-length "Water Lilies" when the museum was closed on my last day there. So, of course, I heartily welcomed the idea!

There were a few challenges involved in planning the wedding. First, how do you plan for something to take place thousands of miles from where you live? Second, where should we go on our honeymoon and third, how do we pay for all of this. I did some research and discovered that there was a company that would provide a celebrant, someone to come to our hotel to do Monica's hair and makeup, a photographer and a chauffeur to take us to the site and drive us around Paris for three hours afterwards while the photographer took photos of us in front of famous monuments. The cost for the package was nominal and quite affordable.

Because of my creative nature, I enjoyed putting together our travel plans. We decided to fly to New York first for a few days to make the trip more manageable. Also, Monica had never been to New York while I had attended college there and knew it quite well. I was happy to be her tour guide. We stayed at a hotel near Central Park and took a horse and carriage ride around the park and had dinner at the "Tavern on the Green". We saw "CATS" at the Neil Simon Theatre on Broadway. We took a cruise around Manhattan that included a view of the Statue of Liberty, my favorite monument in New York. We had dinner with my college friend, Rick, at a wonderful Italian restaurant. Of course, we also had pizza in an area known as "Hell's Kitchen", famous for its pizzerias.

After New York, we flew to Paris. Since we both liked Disneyland and Disneyworld, we decided to visit Disney Paris. Some of the rides were different and the food was a little disappointing considering we were in France, but we still enjoyed the unique experience.

One of the highlights while in Paris included a visit to Monet's former home in Giverny. Of course, it was surrounded by water lilies. We discovered that Monet had a stream diverted to run past his house so he could grow the water lilies and then paint them. Such determination and dedication! He also had a Japanese garden and grew bamboo. Not surprisingly, his house was full of paintings by him as well as other artists. As a cooking aficionado, I enjoyed seeing his French "country kitchen."

Prior to our wedding date, we opted for a package that included a bus tour of the city, a cruise down the Seine and sightseeing at the Eiffel Tower. We found a men's clothing store where I could rent a tux and an ascot. We videotaped the salesperson showing me how to tie the ascot so it would look proper on our wedding day.

Here we are pre-wedding in our attire, me with a properly tied ascot and Monica in her $37 wedding dress from Ross.

"Ready For The Big Event"

Finally, our wedding day on 7/7/17 arrived. We chose this date to make it easier to remember our anniversary and our dear friend, "Auntie Kay" from Hawaii, was going to be in Paris that day as well. It was great having her in attendance and she also took a video of the ceremony for us. As we stood along the Seine, there was a fisherman about 20 yards to our right, tourist cruise ships going down the Seine and people looking down on us from behind and above us. The Eiffel Tower stood majestically behind us as well, just as we planned it. Everything around us faded into the background as my eyes were focused on my beautiful soon-to-be wife, Monica. The event seemed so surreal. Finally, we exchanged rings and then these vows:

I promise that our marriage will be one that glorifies God and puts Him first in our relationship.

I promise to love you for who you are.

I promise to always respect, support and encourage you.

"With This Ring, I Thee Wed"

Once the ceremony ended, people that were overlooking from above us and those in cruise ships on the Seine cheered and clapped for us.

"So Happy Together"

It's now time for the wedding couple's first dance.

"Could I Have This Dance For The Rest of Our Lives?"

We took a little stroll along the Seine and didn't realize the blessing that we were receiving at that time. After we returned home and looked at our photos, we noticed this one had a dove in it as if the Holy Spirit was blessing our marriage. It was as if God was confirming the plans He had for us from when we first met till now and thereafter. This delighted us even more!

"Receiving the Holy Spirit's Blessing"

Across from the Eiffel Tower is a carousel. It seems like a perfect metaphor for marriage. There will always be ups and downs but love will keep it going round and round for many years.

"On A Carousel of Love"

The chauffeur and photographer then took us to various sites around Paris to take our photo. The first stop was at the Louvre.

Road to Utopia

"I Louvre You!"

Next, we went to a spot with Notre Dame in the background.

"Kiss in Front of Iconic Notre Dame"

The last stop was at a typical Parisian cafe where we shared some laughs and how delighted we were to have gotten married in Paris, the "City of Love".

"Can You Believe We Actually Got Married in Paris?"

While still in our wedding attire, we then went to a restaurant to celebrate. Patrons sitting next to us bought us champagne. After dinner, we went back to our hotel where we found that they had placed rose petals on our bed. It was at this point that I could ask Monica, "Voulez-vous Couche Avec Moi, Ce Soi''? Fortunately, she said, "Oui!"

After Paris, we went to Budapest, Hungary, where Monica's mom and grandmother grew up. We stayed at Hotel Boscolo which had ceilings so ornate that it seemed like we were in an art museum. A Hungarian orchestra would play every night while patrons had dinner. Breakfast was buffet-style with multiple food choices consisting of both gourmet and standard fare. Both Hungarian and American coffee were offered. The basement of the hotel had a "relaxation pool" which had subtle blue lighting and soft music. You could do laps or stand by the side for a hot tub effect.

The city of Budapest actually comprises two areas, Buda and Pest, which are separated by the Danube River. Our stay in Budapest included a dinner cruise down the Danube River, a tour of Parliament, Heroes Park with statues of heroic patriots ("the Seven chieftains of the Magyars"), a "Pop-Up" park on some formerly empty grounds and a visit to St. Stephen's Basilica.

One of the interesting highlights of Budapest are their thermal spas. We went to the Szechenyi Medicinal Bath. The water is provided by two thermal springs and the temperature is constant between 74–77 degrees. When we went, there was an elderly man in his 80s playing chess while he was in the water. I decided to challenge him to a game. I was losing at first, then winning, then losing with no hope in sight so I resigned. He was really upset that I wouldn't play it out and give him the satisfaction of checkmating me.

When we were planning our honeymoon trip, Monica suggested that we also go to Italy since we would be right there in Europe. So, after Budapest, we flew to Venice, Italy. We stayed at a small hotel on Lido Island, across the bay from Venice. It was only a 15-minute water taxi ride to Venice and was a lot less expensive and not as congested. The island was only about

2 miles long and 1 mile wide so there was a calm and serene vibe about it.

We discovered limoncello on our journey and realized we liked it. We decided to buy a bottle when we were in Lido and went to a local grocery store. They had four different brands and we weren't sure which one to get. There were four boys in their early 20s standing nearby so we asked them which one was the best. The response we got was, "Just buy the cheapest one because you just want to get drunk, right?" Wrong. Not surprisingly, when we were walking back to our hotel later that night, we saw them on the side of the road and one of them was vomiting. Ah, "la dolce vita!"

We took a train to Pisa and noticed that the tower was still standing and took the obligatory photos of us holding it up.

The last stop on our journey was Florence. On the train from Venice to Florence, another American couple told us that we could purchase leather at very inexpensive prices in Florence. Since we lived in Hawaii at the time, we couldn't imagine wearing leather and didn't think much about the opportunity. However, when we were walking around the market one day, Monica bought a beautiful leather purse, and I bought a briefcase, belt and wallet.

On the last night of our honeymoon in Florence, we decided to take a taxi from the center of the city to Plaza de Michelangelo which was at the top of a hill overlooking the city and where everyone went to see the sun set. Our driver was unusually talkative, but he only spoke Italian. Fortunately, I had Google Translate on my phone so when he spoke, it came out in English and when I spoke, it came out in Italian.

He was surprised that we were from Hawaii and got married in Paris. We mentioned that a lot of people go to Hawaii to get married, and we wanted to do something different. When we told him that we spent time in Venice, he asked if we rode the gondola and, if we did, did the gondolier sing? We said yes and he asked what song he sang. I said, "O Sole Mio". He then proceeded to sing it and asked me to copy him. Basically, I was receiving classical opera training, but I don't think I'm ready for the stage just yet. He sang so well that when we told him that he should be a gondolier instead of a taxi driver, he laughed heartily.

When we reached our destination, he said that "All of Italy is watching us." We weren't quite sure what he meant, and he repeated it. So, I said, "Yes, and so is God."

He said, "No, not Deo, Italy." Then he motioned to some people outside the car, and we noticed they had a boom mike and a microphone. We then noticed the cameras and microphones inside the car. When Monica said, "Oh, so you're a celebrity", he said, "Yes, that's what I've been trying to tell you!"

As it turns out, he was Mika, a famous European singer who sings both opera and pop music, which includes a duet with Ariana Grande, the "Popular Song." He was also a coach on the French version of "The Voice". He hosted an Italian TV show called "Stasera Casa Mika" (Mika's House Tonight) and had a taxi segment on it where he showed clips of him taking unbeknownst passengers on rides. Since we had no clue who he was, we were the perfect passengers.

So, how did we pay for this unforgettable trip? For starters, we had enough frequent flier miles to fly first class in "lie-flat" seats from Honolulu to New York. Then, we could afford to fly business class from New York to Paris. Air travel in Europe is relatively inexpensive compared to the United States.

We researched reasonably priced hotels for the places we stayed. We didn't go overboard eating at restaurants and sometimes brought food from local markets back to our room. We negotiated an excellent price with a gondolier in Venice for just the two of us to ride in the gondola. Overall, the total cost of our three-week extravaganza was less than half of what a traditional wedding in Hawaii would have cost!

MY FINAL THOUGHTS

When we looked at our wedding photos a few months after we returned home, we noticed that in one of them, there was a blue dove hovering over us as we walked along the Seine when the wedding ceremony was over. We immediately realized that this was a sign that the Holy Spirit blessed our wedding and honeymoon!

Then we reflected on all the blessings we received along the way. There was the ability to fly first class from Honolulu to New York for free. When we flew from New York to Paris, a steward put a bottle of champagne in Monica's carry-on bag in the overhead compartment.

The hotel manager in Paris put red rose petals on our bed when we arrived back from our wedding day. At dinner on our wedding night, people next to us bought us champagne, probably because we were still dressed in our wedding attire.

When we arrived at the hotel in Budapest, they upgraded us to a Junior Suite with padded walls and a rooftop lanai.

We received our final, and one of our greatest blessings, when we were flying back home. When we went from

New York to Paris, we enjoyed business class so much that we decided to upgrade the return flight to the same level. We went to the Air France desk and told them our intentions and mentioned that we were in Paris to get married. They told us to wait until we returned later and mentioned that it would be less expensive and there were plenty of seats available at that time.

When we were leaving Florence for Paris, we went to the Air France desk and asked for the upgrade from Paris to New York. We were told that, unfortunately, not only were there no seats available, but they also had to downgrade us from comfort plus to coach. It seemed like such an unfair way to end our honeymoon.

As soon as we landed in Paris, we went back to the Air France desk to complain about the situation. The gentleman helping us did some things on his computer and spoke with his supervisor. Then he told us that we had been upgraded. When I asked, "how much extra do we need to pay?" He said, "Well, you can give me money if you want to but it's free and is already on the computer!" It seemed like the Air France employees in Paris must have made this arrangement when we first requested the change there.

There are kind-hearted souls everywhere in the world!

NOW YOUR TURN

What memories do you have of your wedding and honeymoon?
_____
_____
_____

Was the experience worth the cost?
_____
_____
_____

What would you do differently, if anything?
_____
_____
_____

Would you have preferred a "destination wedding" rather than a traditional wedding?
_____
_____
_____

What factors helped you decide where to go on your honeymoon?
_____
_____
_____

CHAPTER FIFTEEN
FAMILY TIES

O NE OF THE CHALLENGES OF LIVING IN HAWAII WAS that it was so far removed from the continental U.S. It takes five hours just to fly to Los Angeles. My parents and most of my family lived in Michigan, Minnesota, and Wisconsin and it would take another six hours to get there from Los Angeles.

I lived in Hawaii for 14 years. During that period, I pretty much did everything and saw everything I wanted to. I tried surfing to no avail. I was too tired to try standing after paddling all the way out to pick up the surf. I visited all the tourist sites. Pearl Harbor was difficult because it represented such a sad time in U.S. history. I went snorkeling for the first time in 30 years in Hanauma Bay. I even tried eating Hawaiian food. I loved poke and hated poi.

As an insurance broker, I was able to visit all the islands to meet with clients and prospects, at my company's expense. Flights were only around 30 minutes to each of the islands.

One of my clients on Molokai put on a rodeo and I convinced my company to provide financial support. This meant that I had to go and represent my company at the event.

I took photos everywhere I went of waterfalls, volcanoes, sunsets, animals, flowers, cloud formations, etc. Hawaii was, and is, a photographer's paradise. Naturally, I took Monica with me on trips whenever possible. It was always a delight to photograph her beauty surrounded by Hawaii's. The best part of living in Hawaii was meeting and, eventually, marrying Monica.

As an insurance broker, one of my responsibilities was to constantly get new customers. Due to its size and the fact that it's an island, opportunities in this area were extremely limited. I had an extremely high retention rate with my clients, but I was having trouble acquiring new ones. My boss started pressuring me as if I had a magic wand that I could wave, and new clients would magically appear. He replaced my former boss, and his background was in real estate, so he didn't quite understand the insurance industry.

I would call my parents every weekend. Eventually, my dad passed away at the age of 90. After that, whenever I called my mom, her first question would always be, "So, Pete, when are you moving back to Michigan?" My response would be, "I'm sorry, mom, but we just don't like cold weather." However, when my mom turned 90, it started tugging at my heart. It seemed like it was time to move on from my insurance job and, since I didn't know how much longer my mom would be around, I decided that I really needed to move closer to her but, hopefully, somewhere warm.

Having had to look for a new job numerous times in my career, I knew that finding one was a "full-time job" in itself. Therefore, I resigned my position with the insurance broker and set forth on finding a job back in the continental U.S. I looked for one in the warm climates of Southern California, Arizona, Texas and Florida.

Monica suggested that I compile a list of what I was looking for in my next job and then pray about it each night. She also thought I should add "or more" to each item that I was seeking. For example:

- I'm looking for a job closer to my mom and in a warm climate—or more.
- I welcome a salary equal to what I was making—or more.
- I say yes to three weeks vacation like at my last job—or more.

It took eight long months, but I was finally successful and received a job that checked all my prayer boxes. A city in Southern Florida offered me a position as their Risk Manager. They paid to move Monica and me and our possessions across the Pacific Ocean and the mainland. The pay was the same as I made before but the cost of living was so much lower, I ultimately received a healthy increase in pay. I received six weeks of vacation instead of three. And even though we were still a thousand miles from her, my mom was so excited that we were a lot closer and in the same time zone. She told her friends and my extended family that she was so grateful we finally moved back to the United States. To her Hawaii was a different country.

We visited her every year and helped her celebrate her 92nd birthday. When we called her, her voice was always so full of excitement as she would say, "I can't believe I'm 91 (and 92 and 93)!" My goal was always to make her laugh when I called her but, more often than not, she made me laugh.

I get my humor from both of my parents but in different ways. My dad's humor was subtle whereas my mom's humor is more outlandish and uses the element of surprise quite well. I will always remember this about my mom, especially since her last words to me were in the form of a joke. When I called her during her last week and she was still coherent, I told her that I loved her. Her response was, "So, what, you didn't love me before?!"

After I arrived in Florida, I led a worship service at an assisted living home across the street from me once a month. One of their favorite songs that they liked to sing was "I'll Fly Away." During my last phone conversation with my mom, she couldn't speak very well but could hear me. I started singing this song to her and she sang along with me (as best as she could)!

I felt so blessed that my Mom lived to 93 and am so glad that I made the decision to be closer to her in her final years.

MY FINAL THOUGHTS

Being unemployed for eight months was a true test of my faith but I never wavered. I knew that God had a plan for me, and I had to just keep believing in Him and in it.

Family ties can be strong. I am so thankful that God provided a way for me to be closer to my mom and see her in the last years of her life. I'll never forget how excited she was when we would see her or even just talk to her on the phone. She was one of the most caring and giving people I have ever met, and I hope that I am able to continue her legacy while remembering to laugh and bring the joy of laughter to others.

There is more to life than beautiful sunsets. Hawaii is extremely expensive as it costs a fortune to ship goods there. Hawaiians get upset when mainlanders consider them to be a foreign country but living there feels like it is as they focus on preserving their language and many want to return to the old ways when they had kings and queens and could rule themselves.

Soon after moving to Florida, I realized that it was like a "poor man's Hawaii." It has similar attributes like Hawaii does with sunshine, beaches, palm trees, etc. Unlike Hawaii, there is no state income tax, and the cost of living is much lower. My new job in Florida paid me about the same as I earned in Hawaii, but it was like receiving a pay raise since living expenses here were so much lower.

NOW YOUR TURN

Have you ever found yourself torn between living your life's dream and being close to family?

_____
_____
_____

If so, how did you resolve it?

_____
_____
_____

Does "being near family" keep you from moving to a more ideal locale or getting a better job?

_____
_____
_____

What's on your prayer list?

_____
_____
_____

CHAPTER SIXTEEN
RETIREMENT

My job as Risk Manager for the city in Florida that hired me seemed like a dream position. I was responsible for purchasing insurance to protect the city's assets and its employees. I also provided input on safety measures. I wasn't happy with the current broker that we had so I orchestrated a broker selection process and was able to hire a firm that I knew would do an excellent job and they did. We were able to increase our limits while saving money at the same time.

I even convinced the City Council to purchase Umbrella Liability insurance. The Mayor and Assistant Mayor were opposed but it passed on a vote of 7-2. I was able to utilize all the experience I had gained working for over 40 years in insurance and risk management. Then COVID hit and my position was eliminated. Again, I needed to find another job. I wondered why God had provided this job for me after leaving Hawaii and then it was taken away. I relied on my faith that He had a plan for me.

It reminded me of when I first arrived in Hawaii and wondered "why am I here?" This time, I wondered why did God answer my prayers about finding a job close to my mom in a warm climate with better job benefits and then take it away from me. It really magnified the fact that, as humans, quite often we don't understand what God's ultimate plan is for us. We just have to have faith that He knows what's best for us. It wasn't easy, but, that is what I decided to do.

I collected unemployment for six weeks. Then I was able to land a couple of consulting jobs doing risk management. When my funds were about to be fully depleted, I won $5,000 on a lottery scratcher ticket! I couldn't believe it. However, because of COVID, the offices were closed, and I had to either mail it in or go all the way to Tallahassee, which would have taken me at least a whole day to drive there, but most likely more due to breaks and sightseeing. I decided to wait until the offices opened again. Finally, they did, and I quickly went and collected my winnings.

The next day, Monica and I were walking around a park across the street from where we lived. It was empty except for a dad teaching his son how to box. I stopped to chat with him as he was wearing a Pittsburgh Pirates shirt with Roberto Clemente's name on it. He was a contemporary of my favorite player Hank Aaron. We talked about both players for a while and then he said, "By the way, Jesus told me to tell you that He loves you." Tears started welling up immediately and usually whenever I tell someone this story.

Not only did Jesus love me but He, of course, had a plan for me. Soon, I was hired to be the Risk and Safety Manager by a public entity across the state on the Gulf side. I had no idea where that was or what the area was like. I told my friends that I had landed a new job and that I would be working in "Whoville."

At first, I wasn't sure how much I would like to move to that area because it was colder than Hollywood and the salary was a little lower than what I was making for the city. You would think that by now I would not question any of God's plans for me.

The job again provided me with the satisfaction of using everything I learned about risk management and insurance during my career. Initially, I had a good relationship with my boss who, like me, had a great sense of humor. We also communicated very well with each other. The company had several buildings spread out over a campus-style area surrounded by trees. My co-workers and I would take daily walks when it was break time. There was even a basketball hoop and basketballs to help me flash back to the good ol' days.

As the Risk Manager, it was my responsibility to see firsthand the activities that employees would engage in to ascertain the risks and ensure that we were protected by both adequate safety measures and sufficient insurance coverage in case of an accident. This included spending a day in a skiff on Tampa's Bay to analyze seaweed in the water below, watching and taking part in a "controlled burn" of forest area and a drilling operation to determine how low the water table was. The diversity of our operations was very appealing to me.

My wife and I chose to live in a 55+ community. It had a Pickleball court, and I couldn't wait to learn and play the sport. It also had three golf courses and a par-3 course. Although I enjoyed golfing over the years, I didn't have time as I was working full-time and playing pickleball on Wednesday nights and Saturday mornings.

It was both exciting and frustrating living in the community. Exciting because of so many available activities but frustrating because I wasn't always available to take advantage of them.

One event that I could partake in that I thoroughly enjoyed was a monthly "Name That Tune." About 10 seconds of a song would be played and each table of eight had to guess the title, artist and the next line. Since music has always been a big part of my life and with my DJ experience in college, I welcomed the challenge and usually did well. So far, my team has placed 2nd and 3rd out of 25 tables.

There were numerous clubs in the community, and we joined many of them. These included the Pickleball club, Newcomers, and Boomers and many others. Each club had monthly social activities. Pickleball had potlucks where the club provided the main dish and everyone else brought side dishes and whatever they wanted to drink. Newcomers and Boomers provided musical entertainment and we brought food and drinks for our table. One night, the Newcomers' entertainment included a band with the original guitarist for Steppenwolf. It was amazing to see 90-year-old ladies rocking out and dancing to their music!

While my job started out well, things started to sour (again!). I chose five brokers for a broker selection process. I was accused of showing favoritism and having a relationship with one of the brokers since they were selected at my last job. However, because I had worked in the industry for 40 years, I had some sort of relationship with all of them. One of them was the prior broker for the city I worked for. I worked for another one and had solicited proposals from the other two in my last position. It was very confusing to me why we would want to select a broker that we didn't know anything about and hope that they lived up to their promises rather than one we had experience with and knew exactly what we were getting.

One of my responsibilities was to recommend types of insurance and limits that vendors and contractors who worked on our premises were required to have. They needed to provide proof of coverage in case one of their actions caused injury to a third party on our premises at that time. We wanted to be sure that the vendor/contractor had this protection and we wanted to be named as an Additional Insured on their policy. This was so we could forward any claims we received for their actions to their insurance company.

For whatever reason, our project managers weren't always receptive to the insurance requirements that I requested. They would complain to their manager who would complain to my boss's manager who would complain to my manager. As you might expect, my manager would then consult with me to understand my decision.

The last time this occurred, she asked me to explain why I was requiring certain coverage. I explained to her what kind of loss could occur and her response was, "How likely is that to happen?" That was not how risk management was supposed to work. If insurance was only required when there was a better-than-average possibility of a loss occurring, it is unlikely that any insurance would ever be required.

It was not surprising when my boss informed me that my services were no longer required. Since I felt that my boss had a different viewpoint on how risk management should be handled, leaving was mutual.

So, now what? I was turning 72 in a few months, not the ideal age to find another job. After much praying, soul searching and financial analysis, I decided that our household income would be sufficient for me to retire. I felt so relieved when I made this decision. Immediately, a great amount of stress was eliminated in my life. Stress from getting up early even when I didn't feel well. Stress from driving 30 minutes each way to and from work. Stress from job pressures. Most of all, stress from corporate nonsense.

Most people plan when they are going to retire, and their company usually gives them a retirement party. Obviously, that wasn't going to happen in my case, so I threw one myself at a facility in my community. It was important to me to earmark the decision and momentous occasion. Around 30 people attended including my sister and her husband from Michigan.

I started playing pickleball three times a week, went golfing, played ping pong and joined a Bocce Ball league. I was able to spend more time with Monica and we took many trips together, both domestically and internationally. I joined the Players Club and performed in a Radio Readers program and a play, "Murder For Dummies."

There have been days when I didn't remember what day it was and even days when I kept looking for mail not realizing it was a Federal Holiday like Veterans Day. Other times, I didn't feel like getting up to play pickleball at 9:00 a.m. and realized that if I had been working, I would have had to gut it out and go to work. Every day when I wake up, I thank God for all of His blessings and the "Best Life" that I am now enjoying!

MY FINAL THOUGHTS

Jesus loves me. Whenever I needed help in my life, He extended His hand. My last job in my risk management career was in a quaint little town that felt like Big Rapids in a positive way. Once you turn 55, living in a 55 and older community provides many great benefits. Public entities have some bizarre rules that make no sense. You don't need hundreds of thousands of dollars to retire. You just need a positive cash flow.

Before I retired, I asked some friends who had retired what their day was like. I was shocked to hear "I can't believe how busy I am!" Once I retired, I soon found out that this was true. Instead of your day being filled with job responsibilities, it's filled with things that you want to do and enjoy doing.

When I retired, I knew my life would be less stressful due to no longer having to get up early to go to work, commuting to and from work and working eight hours a day each week. What I also soon realized was how much stress was reduced by not having to deal with "Corporate BS". Now, the only stress I encounter is trying to decide whether I want to play pickleball, bocce ball, swim in the pool, relax in the hot tub or write a book.

NOW YOUR TURN

Have you planned out your retirement?
_____
_____
_____

Where do you see yourself retiring?
_____
_____
_____

What do you imagine your life looking like in retirement?
_____
_____
_____

What blessings have you had that has brought you new opportunities in life?
_____
_____
_____

How active do you plan on being in retirement?
_____
_____
_____

CHAPTER SEVENTEEN
UTOPIA

ONE DEFINITION OF *UTOPIA* IS "A PLACE, STATE, OR CONdition that is ideally perfect." However, the literal Greek translation of "outopos" is actually "no place." I understood that to mean since perfection doesn't exist, utopia is going to be different for everyone.

This chapter explores my understanding of where utopia can be found on Earth, in Heaven and in Heaven on Earth.

Where does one find utopia?

If, as God stated in Genesis, "Cursed is the ground because of you; through painful toil you will eat food from it all the days of your life," then where can one find utopia on Earth? After all, my belief is that a person transitions from child to adult when they recognize and accept the harsh reality of life: "*In this world, you will have trouble.*" John 16:33

The answer lies in a person's mindset. You can physically move to where you consider an ideal place to live but it is your state of mind that will allow you to live in a utopian condition.

When we wake up each morning, we have two choices.

- Choice A: We can allow negative situations and circumstances to cloud our perspective.
- Choice B: We can cherish all the positive things that are happening in our life.

God has a plan for each of us and He truly wants us to enjoy life while we are here on earth. That is why I believe He provides miracles for us. We just have to open our eyes to see them.

If your eyes aren't open to seeing them, you might miss the small miracles. These would include things that I have witnessed like finding parking at a crowded spot, seeing and photographing beautiful sunsets or finding something that was once lost.

I've also been blessed with big ones like overcoming polio, finding the love of my life, or winning $5,000 on a lottery ticket when I was out of work.

I've overcome shyness, I completed a marathon and I found a number of jobs when I needed them, which improved my quality of life. I give credit to God for those everyday miracles too.

But, my favorite miracles that He has provided me with include the birth of my children, finding love late in life and the ability to enjoy life in retirement.

Let's review the challenges I have faced in my life and how I overcame them and used them in a positive way on my road to utopia.

- Polio—Although I was only four years old at the time, there had to be an inner desire of mine to overcome the disease to make it happen. Once I overcame it, it freed me to run in and complete a marathon and win speech competitions, both of which provided great pleasure.

- Boredom—While boredom is not fun, it motivated me to create and even relish challenges. Each time this happened, it aroused the fire inside me and brought me enjoyment, regardless of the result.
- Priesthood—While my parents were trying to dictate my future, even though I went in another direction, they guided me down a spiritual path. This eventually culminated with me providing worship service to residents of an assisted living home and focusing on leading others to Christ.
- Shyness—My hypersensitivity led me to a state of extreme shyness which caused social awkwardness. However, by living inside myself, I came to know myself on a deep level and also be sensitive to what other people go through.
- Culture Shock—Yes, I had to go from being a sheltered child to growing up overnight but it heightened my awareness of the real world and taught me important life skills.
- Life or Death—I could have died numerous times. Each time I didn't, I was reminded that God has a plan for me.
- New York City Marathon—I had to overcome many obstacles to completing this race. As painful as it was, it gave me great pleasure knowing that I had finished the race in spite of everything. Going forward, whenever I am faced with a tough task, I always remind myself that I was able to complete a marathon so I should be able to do anything else.
- French Connection—The first time I traveled to a foreign country, it was a little frightening. I no longer felt in my comfort zone as I didn't speak the language, know their culture, and had difficulty doing everyday tasks like putting a plug in a socket. Once I had that experience, it gave me confidence that I could travel again almost anywhere, and I did.
- Creative Outlets—I think my creative talent is one of the best gifts I have been blessed with because I can feel God

working through me when I am using it. I know many creative artists who haven't had opportunities to use their talent. However, it has seemed like opportunities have always presented themselves to me and then I would just let the creativity flow.
- Frostbitten—We each get to choose how we want to live. We are in control of our happiness. I learned early in my life that I didn't like cold weather so I moved to places with warmer temps. I also need a warm relationship with whomever I'm married to. When that didn't happen, I moved on. Both the weather and my first marriage ruined any sense of utopia for me so I took control and continued on my road to utopia.
- Changing Directions—Life, as the Beatles once said, is a *"Long and Winding Road."* It takes you in many different directions. Sometimes a new direction might surprise you. This happened when I went from thinking that I never wanted children to happily being the father to two wonderful daughters. I was very happy living in Southern California for 25 years but, when I needed to find another job, headed to the even warmer climate of Hawaii. After being raised Catholic and then searching for a better spiritual path, I discovered that I wanted Christ in my life and to be a Christian. All of these changes improved my life and I felt like I was definitely going down the right road.
- Delayering—I was not able to work for one company for my entire career. That was due to one of two things. Either my employer no longer believed I was a good fit for the current direction the company was going in or I believed that my employer was no longer a good fit for me. Whenever I left an employer either at their request or my desire, the next position almost always proved to be better.

- Love, At Last—I found that it was best not to limit the possibilities of meeting the love of my life regardless of how old I was. It is all about a mindset. I didn't close myself off to love and found true happiness with my current wife when I was 64.
- Wedding and Honeymoon—Many people like to get married in Hawaii and then honeymoon there. Since we lived there, Monica and I decided to do something else. We both had a desire to go to Paris so that became the plan, a destination wedding. The challenge then became making arrangements for an event that would take place thousands of miles from Hawaii, deciding how to spend our honeymoon and how to pay for everything. We were successful in meeting all of these challenges and even saved over $10,000 from what a traditional wedding in Hawaii would have cost. The trip turned out to be a blessing in every possible way.
- Family Ties—I stayed close to home to go to college the first two years but transferred to a school more than 1,000 miles away from home. I needed to follow my own path. I was torn between staying close to family or pursuing a career that took me a great distance away. My career path followed the latter direction. However, with my dad no longer alive and my mom in her 90s, I had a strong urge to get closer to her geographically. I'm glad I did as I got to see her in her later years and even help her celebrate her 92nd birthday in person!
- Retirement—My life epitomized that of a classic late bloomer. Everything came late to me in life. This was true whether it was biologically, emotionally, physically and even maturity-wise. It also affected my career. Because of all the delayering that I went through, I could not afford to retire at age 65, 66, 67 all the way through age 71. Finally, as I approached my

72nd birthday, I realized that it was now a possibility and leaped into retirement! I am now living the best years of my life which certainly has an utopian feel about it.

As I described in the beginning of this chapter, the key to finding utopia is not only in where one chooses to live but also that person's mindset. I moved to warm locales like Southern California, Hawaii and Florida but also my mindset was to find the positive in every situation and encounter. Both of these attributes have led me to find utopia on Earth.

Once we leave Earth, most of us desire to enter Heaven for life after death and a greater sense of utopia. Those who believe that Jesus Christ was the Son of God and was sent to Earth to die for our sins believe that there is life after death. John 11:25-26 states that Jesus said:

> *"I am the resurrection and the life. Those who believe in me, even though they die, will live, and everyone who lives and believes in me will never die."*

In John 14:1-3, Jesus also promised that we would be with Him in Heaven:

> *"Do not let your hearts be troubled. Trust in God: trust also in me. In my Father's house are many rooms; if it were not so, I would have told you. I am going there to prepare a place for you. And if I go and prepare a place for you, I will come back and take you to be with me that you also may be where I am."*

What will our bodies be like once we get to Heaven?

> *"Christ will transform our lowly bodies so that they will be like His glorious body." Philippians 3:21.*

Furthermore, we will experience even greater utopia than here on Earth as we will no longer endure pain and suffering as it has been told in Revelations 21:1-4:

> *"He will dwell with them, and they shall be His people, and God himself will be with them; He will wipe away every tear from their eyes, and death shall be no more, neither shall there be mourning nor crying nor pain any more, for the former things have passed away."*

Yes, we will experience an even greater utopia than what we could have on Earth when we are in Heaven. However, this will not be our final destination nor our greatest utopia. That will be what we will experience when God has restored Heaven on Earth. This will occur after the period of tribulation as described in the book of Revelations. It is described by John in this book in Revelations 21:1-4:

> *"Then I saw a new heaven and a new earth, for the old heaven and the old earth had disappeared. And the sea was also gone. And I saw the holy city, the new Jerusalem, coming down from God out of heaven like a beautiful bride prepared for her husband.*
>
> *I heard a loud shout from the throne, saying, "Look, the home of God is now among his people! He will live with them, and they will be his people. God himself will be with them. He will remove all of their sorrows, and there will be no more death or sorrow or crying or pain. For the old world and its evils are gone forever."*

Who will experience this utopia? All who believe that Jesus is our savior and are sorry for their sins. Revelations 21: 7-8 further states:

> "All who are victorious will inherit all these blessings, and I will be their God, and they will be my children. But cowards who turn away from me, and unbelievers, and the corrupt, and murders, and the immoral, and those who practice witchcraft, and idol worshippers, and all liars — their doom is in the lake that burns with fire and sulfur."

If you do not know where you are going when you die and/or have not accepted Jesus in your life but wish to enjoy the blessings described above, please know that:

> "For God so loved the world, that He gave His only begotten Son, that whosoever believeth in Him should not perish, but have everlasting life." John 3:16

Also:

> "If you confess with your mouth that Jesus is Lord, and believe in your heart that God has raised Him from the dead, you will be saved." Romans 10:9

If you do seek salvation, please say this prayer out loud:

> "Dear Lord Jesus, I know that I am a sinner, and I ask for Your forgiveness. I believe You died for my sins and rose from the dead. I turn from my sins and invite You to come into my heart and life. I want to trust and follow You as my Lord and Savior. In Your Name. Amen."

If you do this, you will be accepting the greatest gift that you could ever receive. I pray that you are filled with the Holy Spirit who will guide you and help you overcome any hesitation in moving in this direction. God bless you. Amen.

MY FINAL THOUGHTS

Everyone has their own definition of what utopia is like here on Earth. However, it is limited by things that we can not control and determined by how we approach life with all the challenges we will endure.

My hope is that my presentation of how I dealt with the many challenges I have encountered will help you deal with yours. I also hope that you know where you are going when you leave this world so that you can enjoy the glory of Heaven and then later, that of Heaven on Earth.

If you need guidance in this area, here are suggested religious organizations to check out:

One Love Ministries
Honolulu, HI
onelove.org

Oceanside Calvary
Oceanside, CA
calvaryoceanside.org

Life Church
Spring Hill, FL
lifechurchnow.com

Crossroads Bible Church
Grand Rapids, MI
crossroads-bible.org

NOW YOUR TURN

Have you found whatever your definition of utopia is in this world?

_____
_____
_____
_____

Do you know where you're going when you leave this world?

_____
_____
_____
_____

Does "Heaven on Earth" sound like the ultimate utopia to you?

_____
_____
_____
_____

If you haven't already accepted salvation, are you ready now?

_____
_____
_____
_____

ACKNOWLEDGMENTS

THANK YOU TO THE FOLLOWING PEOPLE WHO SUPPORTED me and believed in this creation of mine:

Carrie Severson, for her developmental edit and guidance throughout the publishing process for my book. Her insights definitely upgraded the quality of the book.

Fellow authors Cheryl Ricker, Michele Eisch and Fran Capo for their inspiration in writing this book.

My grandma, who told me to follow my dream when I retired from the insurance industry to pursue a career in Hollywood during the mid-80s. She also told me to be like her and, when I fall down, to get up and climb back up the mountain.

My parents, who helped support me in overcoming polio, instilled in me my faith, and gave me a wonderful sense of humor.

My brother, Allen, who was such a joy to have as a brother and who left a lasting impression of his boldness. "I love you, man!"

My sister Sally for feedback on some chapters of my book and all my sisters, including Kathy, Dorothy Jean, and Gloria, for their love and support over the years.

My daughters, Melissa and Jessica, for all the joy and pleasure they have brought to my life.

Pastor Waxer, whose altar call led me to accepting Jesus and for his two years of discipleship.

Uncle Jay, for his dedication to Common Grace and his inspiration that led me to mentor a student in need of a friend.

Dennis, for providing me with an opportunity to enrich each of our lives by mentoring him from first grade through fifth grade and his continuing friendship thereafter.

Josiah, for his spiritual messages and inspiration.

Pastor Roberto (and his father) for feedback on Chapter 17 and for guiding my current walk with God.

Jack, fellow classmate, travel guide/interpreter in France, Scrabble aficionado, the "Dr. J" to my "Pistol" on the basketball court and someone who is on the same sense of humor wavelength. Also, for providing me with the Greek definition of utopia.

Big Rapids High School (BRHS) Class of '68 for friendships developed over time.

Auntie Kay, our Hawaiian friend, who coordinated her travel to be in Paris on the day that we got married and took a video of the ceremony for us.

Stephanie Bobault, photographer, who provided Monica and me with the wonderful photos she took of us in Paris on our wedding day.

Asparis Driver, our chauffeur who drove us to all the photo sites on our wedding day and also used my cellphone to take additional pictures of us.

Mika, our taxi driver in Florence who included us on the taxi segment of his Italian TV show.

Monica, my wonderful wife, for her love and always challenging me to grow by going outside my comfort zone. Also, for her matching spirit of adventure as we embrace together all the wonders that life has to offer on our road to utopia.

ABOUT THE AUTHOR

Peter Junker is an author who needs and loves challenges so much that God gave him as many as possible. One such challenge that Peter accepted was to write a book about what he has endured and how he has met these challenges in hopes that it would help others who have similar circumstances. This book also provides Peter with the opportunity to express his sense of humor which is one of his favorite gifts. He enjoys making people laugh as well as helping them grow. He is living his best life with the love of his life in Florida. You can email him through his web site at www.pfjconsulting.com.

Milton Keynes UK
Ingram Content Group UK Ltd.
UKHW050001211024
449919UK00017B/191